Dispensationalism

Essential Beliefs
and Common Myths

Revised and Updated

Dispensationalism

Essential Beliefs
and Common Myths

Revised and Updated

Michael J. Vlach

Theological Studies Press
Los Angeles, California

Vlach, Michael, 1966 –
    Dispensationalism / Michael J. Vlach

ISBN 13: 978-0-9798539-2-0
ISBN 10: 0-9798539-2-3

Printed in the United States of America

All Scripture quotations, unless otherwise indicated, are taken from the New American Standard Bible®, Copyright © 1960, 1962, 1963, 1968, 1971, 1972, 1973, 1975, 1977, 1995 by the Lockman Foundation. Used by permission (www.Lockman.org).

Printed in the United States of America

Contents

Preface

The contents of this book are a revision and update to the original 2008 version. The basic structure and content remain yet additional information has been added to each of the chapters. Plus, there are three new chapters: (1) "Continuity and Discontinuity in Dispensationalism"; (2) "Key Differences between Dispensationalism and Covenant Theology"; and (3) "Recommended Sources on Dispensationalism." This revised and updated version offers approximately thirty-five additional pages from the original version.

Introduction

Many of the beliefs of dispensationalism reach deeply into church history. But the system of theology known as dispensationalism began in the mid-nineteenth century. Since its inception it has been popular yet controversial. In addition to millions who have adopted dispensational beliefs, many schools, colleges, seminaries, books, and radio and television teachers have promoted dispensational theology. With great popularity, though, has come significant criticism. Covenant theologians and other non-dispensationalists have offered strong criticisms of dispensationalism at times.

Sometimes the criticisms have been harsh. Some try to link dispensationalism with date setting for Jesus' return. Dispensationalism also has been accused of promoting a false gospel, teaching heresy, and advocating lawless living. Some claim dispensational beliefs lead to lack of concern for global issues such as the threat of nuclear war and diminishing natural resources. Others claim dispensationalism is hurting peace in the Middle East and plunging the world toward Armageddon and global annihilation. Dispensationalism has been criticized for its views on Bible interpretation, the distinction between Israel and the church, and a pre-tribulational rapture of the church. Are these criticisms cause for concern? I do not think they are.

Erroneous information concerning dispensationalism often has been promoted. Three books, for example, have misrepresented dispensationalism—John Gerstner's 1991 book, *Wrongly Dividing the Word of Truth*; Hank Hanegraaff's 2007 book, *Apocalypse Code*; and Keith A. Mathison's 1995 work, *Dispensationalism: Rightly Dividing the People of God*? All three offered misleading presentations of dispensationalism, focusing on matters that are not at the heart of dispensationalism. As I discuss dispensationalism with people I still find it necessary to address false conceptions such as those promoted by these books. Gerstner and Mathison tied dispensationalism with erroneous views regarding salvation, when in reality dispensationalism is primarily about other matters such as hermeneutics, the church, and end times. Gerstner in particular attacked dispensationalism in a highly polemical and confrontational way. Hanegraaff used emotional rhetoric linking dispensationalism to racism, ethnic cleansing, and threats to the deity of Christ. He also connected dispensationalism with the Jehovah's Witnesses, Joseph Smith of Mormonism, Darwinian evolution, and Bill Clinton—people and cults that get a strong negative reaction from Christians.[1] Kim Riddlebarger, an amillennialist who agrees with much of Hanegraaff's eschatology, noted the ungracious tone of the book: "The result is, in my opinion, Hanegraaff's book has a 'snotty,' condescending and sensationalist tone to it."[2]

For some critics, dispensationalism is not just a perspective gone awry on some points—it is dangerous! It threatens the gospel of Jesus Christ! It promotes lawless living! It threatens the deity of Christ! If unchecked it leads to racism and ethnic cleansing! It threatens the world itself! It has much in common with the cults!

---

[1] See Hank Hanegraaff, *The Apocalypse Code: Find out What the Bible Really Says About the End Times and Why It Matters Today* (Nashville, TN: Thomas Nelson, 2007). See pages 38, 70, 44, 124. Hanegraaff also favorably uses a quote that describes premillennialists as "the socially disinherited, psychologically disturbed, and theologically naïve" (44). According to Hanegraaff, today's dispensationalists threaten the entire human race. They are "bent on ensuring that the horrors of Armageddon become a self-fulfilling prophecy" (47). In fact, the only way to save the world according to Hanegraaff is to reject Dispensationalism: "If the evangelical death march toward the endgame of Armageddon is to be subverted, it will be because believers recommit themselves to *faithful illumination*" (48).

[2] Kim Riddlebarger, "Hanegraaff's 'The Apocalypse Code,'" August 15, 2007. http://kimriddlebarger.squarespace.com/the-latest-post/2007/8/15/hanegraaffs-the-apocalypse-code.html?currentPage=2. Accessed March 10, 2017.

Fortunately, not all non-dispensationalists have adopted this scorched-earth approach. Some disagree with dispensationalism but still put the issues into perspective and admit that the battle over dispensationalism is not a battle over the heart of Christianity itself. Vern Poythress's book, *Understanding Dispensationalists*, is an example of a work that is critical of dispensationalism but does so in a respectful manner that focuses on real issues.[1] Covenant theologian, O. Palmer Robertson, also showed a gracious and proper perspective when he wrote:

> As the dispensational perspective is being evaluated, it should not be forgotten that covenant theologians and dispensationalists stand side by side in affirming the essentials of the Christian faith. Very often these two groups within Christendom stand alone in opposition to the inroads of modernism, neo-evangelicalism, and emotionalism. Covenant theologians and dispensationalists should hold in highest regard the scholarly and evangelical productivity of one another. It may be hoped that continuing interchange may be based on love and respect.[2]

Yet because of certain books against dispensationalism that do not offer reasonable and honest presentations, there is a need to respond. This brief book is an attempt to identify the foundational issues of dispensationalism and expose common myths about this theology. Or to put it another way—my aim is to discuss what dispensationalism is and what it is not.

This book is purposely short, functioning much like a "fast facts" about dispensationalism. It focuses on issues most crucial for understanding dispensationalism. It does not address every issue related to dispensational theology. For example, it is not about explaining the traditional seven dispensations of dispensationalism. Nor is it a history of John Nelson

---

[1] Vern S. Poythress, *Understanding Dispensationalists* (P&R Publishing, 1993).

[2] O. Palmer Robertson, *The Christ of the Covenants* (Phillipsburg NJ: Presbyterian and Reformed Publishing, 1980), 201–202.

Darby, who is often viewed as the father of systematized dispensationalism. Instead, this is a short primer that helps people understand what dispensational theology is mostly about, particularly as it exists now in the twenty-first century. Thus, I hope this book can be helpful for both dispensationalists and non-dispensationalists, as well as those trying to make up their minds about dispensationalism.

I think it is possible to define the essential beliefs of dispensationalism. Although there are theological differences among dispensationalists, we can identify core beliefs shared by most dispensationalists. Likewise, we also can identify issues that are often mistakenly viewed as essential to dispensationalism but in reality are not. That is what this book will attempt to do. *It will highlight the foundational beliefs of dispensationalism that truly are at the heart of the system. It will also look at misrepresentations of dispensationalism.*

Such an endeavor must properly take into account the various views within dispensationalism. Not all dispensationalists believe the same thing on every issue. Debated issues include how to define the church, the relationship of the church to the new covenant, and Jesus' relationship to David's throne. Some believe these differences are minor while others hold that they are more serious.

Also there are different camps. Some dispensationalists consider themselves "classical" or "traditional." Others say they are "modified," "revised," or "progressive." Some see themselves incorporating elements from the different variations. Some do not like to use titles at all.

In case you are wondering, on the dispensational spectrum I consider myself between revised and progressive dispensationalism. Yet even as I say that I have a healthy respect for traditional dispensationalism and own much of what traditional dispensationalism affirms. I consider myself as one who has learned much from traditional, revised, and progressive dispensationalists and do not view any of these varieties as an opponent. I often attend meetings with representatives from these three camps and will continue to do so.

In addition, this book is not an attempt to iron out all the points of difference between the variations within dispensationalism. Those looking for a detailed discussion of the differences between the dispensational camps will need to look elsewhere. I recommend the book, *Three Central Issues in Contemporary Dispensationalism: A Comparison of Traditional & Progressive Views*, edited by Herbert W. Bateman.[3] Instead, I am looking to give the reader a basic introduction to the foundational beliefs of dispensational theology as a whole, so a better understanding of this theology can occur.

Whether you are a dispensationalist yourself, an opponent of dispensationalism, or an interested observer trying to gather facts about this theology, it is important to have a correct understanding. The cause of truth is never served by confusion, misrepresentations, and strawman arguments. Most critiques of dispensationalism from non-dispensationalists do not accurately portray what dispensationalism is. There are exceptions to this but unfortunately those who criticize dispensationalism often focus on wrong things or show a lack of understanding about this theology. On the other hand, those who promote dispensationalism have not always been clear either, so the blame is not all one-sided. Sometimes, dispensationalists have not been clear or have presented secondary areas of dispensational doctrine as essential. Personally, I cringe a little bit when I see dispensationalists I respect leading off with complicated discussions of seven dispensations, not because dispensations are not important, but because I think there are other issues that are more foundational to the dispensational perspective.

As you probably now know I am a dispensationalist. Yet I did not grow up in a dispensational environment. I grew up Roman Catholic. When I became a Christian at age 14 I attended churches that held to dispensational beliefs. My main allegiance as a Christian, though, is to the Lord Jesus Christ

---

[3] Herbert W. Bateman IV, ed. *Three Central Issues in Contemporary Dispensationalism: A Comparison of Traditional & Progressive Views* (Grand Rapids: Kregel, 1999).

and His Word. I do not consider myself unconditionally or uncritically bound to any system of theology. In my life I have come out of other theological traditions that I found to be unscriptural and I would do so for dispensationalism if I thought it were unbiblical. But I have not found this to be the case. I have, however, made modifications within my dispensational understanding. As my knowledge of God's Word grows, I find myself making adjustments to line up with what God has revealed.

In case you are interested, my office has no prophecy charts on the wall (although I have nothing against these). While I believe the issue of dispensations is important, the seminary theology classes I teach spend little time discussing the necessity of believing in "seven dispensations," which is not really at the heart of dispensationalism. I do not believe that literal hermeneutics requires believing that trees will literally clap their hands (Isa. 55:12). I also don't view every earthquake and natural disaster as the fulfillment of Bible prophecy. I do believe the reinstitution of the state of Israel in 1948 is theologically significant but I do not dates set concerning the return of Christ. Personally, I think the perception that dispensationalism leads to date-setting for the return of Jesus is way overblown and mostly a straw man characterization. But I want to reaffirm that no person knows when the events associated with Jesus' return and the Day of the Lord will happen.

I appreciate the life and works of the founder of modern dispensationalism, John Nelson Darby, but I do not view my beliefs as unconditionally tied to him. Thus attacks on Darby, many of which are unfounded or out of context,[4] mean little to me since my beliefs in dispensationalism were never linked with Darby to begin with. They have come from my own study of Scripture and learning from other Bible scholars.

---

[4] For an excellent treatment concerning the life and beliefs of John Darby, including a refutation of many false ideas about him, see Paul Wilkinson, *For Zion's Sake: Christian Zionism and the Role of John Nelson Darby*, in Studies in Evangelical History and Thought (Paternoster, 2007).

The reader should note that this work is not a comprehensive treatment of dispensationalism. Charles Ryrie's *Dispensationalism*, and Craig Blaising and Darrell Bock's book, *Progressive Dispensationalism* offer much more detail than this small book does and I recommend reading these works as well.

In sum, this book is my attempt to define what dispensationalism is and what it is not in a relatively short presentation. I have written books much longer than this one but purposely want it to be brief. Also, I do not claim to speak for all dispensationalists, and certainly some would state some matters differently than I do. I firmly believe, though, that what I present here is consistent with what most dispensationalists believe and is a fair representation of dispensationalism.

1

History of Dispensationalism

A discussion of dispensationalism should include a brief survey of its history. As a theological system that offers detailed explanations of ecclesiology (church) and eschatology (end times), dispensationalism is a relatively new theology, beginning in the early-middle nineteenth century. Like its rival, covenant theology, which is an early seventeenth century development,[1] dispensationalism is a post-Reformation system, although many of its ideas have links to the early church.

Also, key ideas associated with dispensationalism, such as premillennialism, hope for a national restoration of Israel, and even pre-tribulationism, were held in the seventeenth and eighteenth centuries. In his groundbreaking book, *Dispensationalism before Darby*, William C. Watson documents conclusively a strong apocalyptic hope similar to dispensationalism that existed in the seventeenth and eighteenth centuries among important English theologians.[2] When dispensationalism comes on the scene it is riding the wave of strong expectations concerning the nation Israel that other theologians were promoting.

Following in this line of pro-national Israel thinking, the origin of systematized dispensationalism is linked with John

---

[1] To be precise, covenant theology first began to form in the late sixteenth century.

[2] William C. Watson, *Dispensationalism Before Darby: Seventeenth-Century and Eighteenth-Century English Apocalypticism* (Silverton, OR: Lampion Press, 2015).

Nelson Darby (1800–1882), a Plymouth Brethren minister. While at Trinity College in Dublin (1819), Darby came to believe in a future salvation and restoration of the nation Israel. Based on his study of Isaiah 32, Darby concluded that Israel, in a future dispensation, will enjoy earthly blessings that were different from the heavenly blessings to be experienced by the church. He saw a clear distinction between Israel and the church. Darby also came to believe in an "any moment" rapture of the church that would be followed by Daniel's Seventieth Week when Israel would once again take center stage in God's plan. After this period, Darby believed there would be a millennial kingdom when God would fulfill His unconditional promises with Israel.[3]

According to Paul Enns, "Darby advanced the scheme of dispensationalism by noting that each dispensation places man under some condition; man has some responsibility before God. Darby also noted that each dispensation culminates in failure."[4] Darby saw seven dispensations: (1) Paradise to the Flood; (2) Noah; (3) Abraham; (4) Israel; (5) Gentiles; (6) The Spirit; and (7) The Millennium. By his own testimony, Darby says his dispensational theology was fully formed by 1833. Darby is often considered the 'father of dispensationalism,' although, as mentioned, Darby certainly was not the first to hold many of the ideas he promoted.

Dispensationalism took shape in the Brethren Movement in early nineteenth century Britain. Those within the Brethren Movement rejected a special role for ordained clergy and stressed the spiritual giftedness of ordinary believers to teach and admonish each other from Scripture. The Brethren had

---

[3] See Floyd Elmore, "Darby, John Nelson," *Dictionary of Premillennial Theology*, Mal Couch, ed., (Grand Rapids: Kregel, 1996), 83–84.

[4] Paul Enns, *The Moody Handbook of Theology* (Chicago: Moody, 1989), 516.

significant influence on evangelical Protestantism and influenced ministers in the United States such as D. L. Moody, James Brookes, J. R. Graves, A. J. Gordon, and C. I. Scofield.[5] Beginning in the 1870s, various Bible conferences were held in the United States. These conferences helped spread dispensationalism. The Niagara conferences (1870–early 1900s) were not started to promote dispensationalism but dispensational ideas were often discussed. The American Bible and Prophetic Conferences from 1878–1914 promoted a dispensational theology. In the late 1800s, several Bible institutes were founded that taught dispensational theology including The Nyack Bible Institute (1882), The Boston Missionary Training School (1889), and The Moody Bible Institute (1889).

C. I. Scofield, a participant in the Niagara conferences, produced the *Scofield Reference Bible* in 1909. This reference Bible became a significant distributor of dispensational theology and put a Bible with dispensational notes in the hands of many. Even critics of dispensationalism still refer to the *Scofield Reference Bible* as the standard bearer of dispensational beliefs.

After World War I many dispensational Bible schools were formed. Led by Dallas Theological Seminary (1924), dispensationalism was promoted in formal, academic settings. Under Scofield, dispensationalism entered a scholastic period that was later carried on by his successor, Lewis Sperry Chafer. Further promotion of dispensationalism took place with Chafer's eight-volume *Systematic Theology* which he finished in 1947. This work was the first comprehensive dispensational theology put together into a single format. It became very popular, going through several reprints.

Variations within Dispensationalism

Dispensationalism has core beliefs held by the vast majority of dispensationalists. One notable belief concerns a future

---

[5] See Craig A. Blaising and Darrell L. Bock, *Progressive Dispensationalism* (Wheaton, IL: Victor, 1993), 10.

salvation and restoration of national Israel. Yet, like other systems of theology, dispensationalism has seen changes and development. As Craig Blaising has pointed out, "Dispensationalism has not been a static tradition."[6] There is no creed or confession that freezes its theological development in history. Through self-analysis and vetting, dispensationalism often has revised itself. Although not everyone classifies the variations within dispensationalism the same way, there have been three key periods in the history of this theology.[7]

Classical Dispensationalism

The "golden age" of dispensationalism began in the 1830s and lasted through the 1940s. This was the era of "classical dispensationalism." Classical dispensationalism refers to the dispensational views of British and American dispensationalists between the writings of John Nelson Darby and Lewis Sperry Chafer's *Systematic Theology* (1947). The interpretive notes of the *Scofield Reference Bible* (1909, 1917) are often seen as the key representation of classical dispensationalism.[8]

One important feature of classical dispensationalism was its dualistic purposes for the peoples of God. God is seen as pursuing two different purposes. One is related to heaven and the other to the earth. As Blaising points out, the "heavenly humanity was to be made up of all the redeemed from all dispensations who would be resurrected from the dead. Whereas the earthly humanity concerned people who had not died but who were preserved by God from death, the heavenly humanity was made up of all the saved who had died, whom God would resurrect from the dead."[9] Blaising also notes that the heavenly, spiritual, and individualistic nature of the church in

---

6 Ibid., 21.

7 Our classification relies on the insights of Craig Blaising in *Progressive Dispensationalism*.

8 Blaising and Bock, 22.

9 Ibid., 24.

classical dispensationalism underscored the well-known view that the church is a *parenthesis* in the history of redemption.[10] With classical dispensationalism there is a very sharp distinction between Israel and the church—so much so that the church and Israel do not even share the same eternal destiny. The church is destined for heaven while Israel will inherit the earth. Dispensationalists of the classical variety sometimes held that there were two new covenants—one for Israel (Jer. 31:31–34) and one for the church (Heb. 8:8–12). Some also held to a distinction between the kingdom of God and the kingdom of heaven. Also, some believed the Sermon on the Mount was only relevant to the coming millennial kingdom and had very little applicability to the church.

Classical dispensationalism could also be called traditional dispensationalism.

Revised or Modified Dispensationalism

The era of revised or modified dispensationalism dates approximately from 1950–1985. After Chafer, revised dispensationalists brought some modifications to classical dispensational theology including a loosening of some of the sharper distinctions between Israel and the church. While still affirming the Israel-church distinction, revised dispensationalists did not emphasize the eternal dualism and separation of heavenly and earthly peoples like classical dispensationalists did. Yet they did emphasize there were two distinct anthropological groups—Israel and the church, which are always kept distinct. These two groups are structured differently with different dispensational roles and responsibilities, but the salvation they each receive and their destination is the same.

For most revised dispensationalists there is one new covenant, not two. The church currently participates in the new covenant while Israel will experience the full fulfillment of the

10 Ibid., 27.

new covenant in a future earthly millennium. The distinction between Israel and the church as different groups will continue throughout eternity even though both groups inherit the millennial kingdom and the eternal state. Also, revised dispensationalists hold that Jesus is not sitting on or ruling from David's throne during the church age. Thus, Jesus' Davidic reign is future. Key theologians of revised dispensationalism include John Walvoord, Dwight Pentecost, Charles Ryrie, Charles Feinberg, and Alva J. McClain. There are many revised dispensationalists today.

Progressive Dispensationalism

The mid-1980s witnessed the rise of progressive dispensationalism. Often linked with the inauguration of the Dispensational Study Group in 1986, progressive dispensationalism offered further modifications to dispensational theology. What does "progressive" refer to? The title "progressive dispensationalism" refers to the "progressive" relationship of the successive dispensations to one another.[11] Charles Ryrie notes that, "The adjective 'progressive' refers to a central tenet that the Abrahamic, Davidic, and new covenants are being progressively fulfilled today (as well as having fulfillments in the millennial kingdom)."[12] With progressive dispensationalism, there is real fulfillment of the covenants of promise in this age. This applies mostly to the spiritual aspects of the new covenant including the indwelling Holy Spirit and Gentile inclusion in the people of God.

Another key belief of progressive dispensationalism concerns the church. According to Craig Blaising and Darrell Bock the church is not a distinct people group in contrast to Israel and Gentiles, but redeemed humanity in this current dispensation:

---

[11] Ibid., 49.

[12] Charles C. Ryrie, "Update on Dispensationalism," *Issues in Dispensationalism*, eds. John R. Master and Wesley R. Willis (Chicago: Moody, 1994), 20.

Progressives do not view the church as an anthropological category in the same class as terms like Israel, Gentile Nations, Jews, and Gentile people. The church is neither a separate race of humanity (in contrast to Jews and Gentiles) nor a competing nation alongside Israel and Gentile nations. . . . The church is precisely redeemed humanity itself (both Jews and Gentiles) as it exists in this dispensation prior to the coming of Christ.[13]

Both Israel and the church compose the "people of God" when it comes to salvation and both are related to the blessings of the new covenant. This spiritual equality, however, does not mean believing Gentiles become "Israel" like non-dispensational systems usually claim. Ethnic identities still exist within the broader concept of the people of God. Also, Israel will have a functional role of leadership and service to the nations when Jesus comes to reign upon the earth (Isa. 2:2–4). This will occur in the millennium.

Also, progressive dispensationalists like Blaising and Bock see an already/not yet aspect to the Davidic throne and Davidic reign of Christ, viewing the Davidic reign as being inaugurated during the present church age. Robert L. Saucy appears to take a mediating view saying there is a sense in which Jesus is exalted to David's throne in heaven, but Jesus is not yet reigning from David's throne. He will do this when He returns to earth. But for all progressive dispensationalists the full fulfillment of this Davidic reign awaits Israel in the millennium. As indicated above, key theologians of progressive dispensationalism include Craig A. Blaising, Darrell L. Bock, and Robert L. Saucy.

There can be a mix of these categories. At the time of this writing many dispensationalists seem to hold to elements of both revised and progressive dispensationalism. There is a growing belief that spiritual aspects of the Abrahamic and new

---

13 Blaising and Bock, 49.

covenants are being fulfilled today, thus real covenant fulfillment is occurring in this present age. This is consistent with a
progressive view. Yet many who hold this do not see enough
support for the idea that Jesus is currently sitting upon and
reigning from David's throne. Progressive dispensationalists
have struggled in convincing other dispensationalists concerning the Davidic throne and reign issue. Most dispensationalists
still believe Jesus' session at the right hand of the Father according to Psalm 110:1 concerns the throne of deity, not David's throne. The Davidic throne assumption and reign awaits
Jesus' second coming (Matt. 19:28; 25:31; Rev. 3:21).

2

Essential Beliefs of Dispensationalism

What are the essential beliefs of dispensationalism—beliefs upon which this theology stands or falls? To help answer this, we can look to how dispensationalists have addressed this issue. I will then offer my own list of foundational beliefs I believe are at the heart of dispensationalism.

In 1965 Charles Ryrie offered three defining marks that he considered to be the essentials or *sine qua non* of dispensationalism: (1) a distinction between Israel and the church; (2) literal interpretation to all Scripture, including prophecy; and (3) the underlying purpose of God in the world is the glory of God.[1] Ryrie's *sine qua non* was well received by most dispensationalists and was often used as a starting point for explaining dispensationalism. Opponents of dispensationalism also used these as starting points for critiquing dispensational theology.

In 1988, with his important chapter, "Systems of Discontinuity," John Feinberg offered six "Essentials of Dispensationalism": (1) belief that the Bible refers to multiple senses of terms like "Jew" and "seed of Abraham"; (2) an approach to hermeneutics that emphasizes that the Old Testament be taken on its own terms and not reinterpreted in light of the New Testament; (3) belief that Old Testament promises will be fulfilled with national Israel; (4) belief in a distinctive future for ethnic Israel; (5) belief that the church is a distinctive organism; and

---

[1] Charles C. Ryrie, *Dispensationalism Today* (Chicago: Moody, 1965), 43–47.

(6) a philosophy of history that emphasizes not just soteriological and spiritual issues but social, economic, and political issues as well.[2]

Although not giving a list of "essentials," Craig Blaising and Darrell Bock offered a list of "common features" of dispensationalism in their 1993 book, *Progressive Dispensationalism*. These features included: (1) the authority of Scripture; (2) dispensations; (3) uniqueness of the church; (4) practical significance of the universal church; (5) significance of biblical prophecy; (6) futurist premillennialism; (7) imminent return of Christ; and (8) a national future for Israel.[3]

Not all of the characteristics mentioned in the above lists, particularly those of Blaising and Bock, are unique to dispensationalism. Many non-dispensationalists, for instance, believe in the authority of Scripture, dispensations, and the significance of biblical prophecy. Some non-dispensationalists also believe in premillennialism—holding that a future millennial kingdom will be established with the second coming of Christ. George Ladd, for instance, held to historic premillennialism, while arguing against dispensational premillennialism. Thus, being a premillennialist does not necessarily mean one is a dispensationalist. It is true, though, that all dispensationalists are premillennialists.

Ryrie's claim that a defining mark of dispensationalism is belief that the underlying purpose of God in the world is the glory of God has been controversial. When properly understood, Ryrie correctly pointed out that dispensationalists often have a broader understanding of God's purposes in the world than some non-dispensationalists who often focus mostly on salvation. Salvation is immensely important, but human salva-

---

[2] John S. Feinberg, "Systems of Discontinuity," *Continuity and Discontinuity: Perspectives on the Relationship Between the Old and New Testaments*, ed. John S. Feinberg (Wheaton, IL: Crossway, 1988), 67–85.

[3] Craig A. Blaising and Darrell L. Bock, *Progressive Dispensationalism: An Up-To-Date Handbook of Contemporary Dispensational Thought* (Wheaton, IL: Bridgepoint, 1993), 13–21.

tion is part of God's broader kingdom purposes. The reconciliation of all things involves everything in the universe as Colossians 1:15–20 indicates.[4] I think dispensationalism has better accounted for this truth.

But the wording Ryrie offered was not the best. Many non-dispensationalists take the glory of God seriously, and to them Ryrie seemed to claim that dispensationalists valued the glory of God more than non-dispensationalists. This was akin to waving a red flag in front of a bull since non-dispensationalists also highly value the glory of God. So while there was a sense in which Ryrie was correct, the way his point was stated did not bring clarity.

I personally do not bring up the glory of God as a distinguishing characteristic of dispensational theology. I believe John Feinberg was more precise when he pointed out that dispensationalists have adopted a philosophy of history that is more holistic and emphasizes more the spiritual and physical implications of eschatology than non-dispensationalists often do. Dispensationalists emphasize the complete and literal fulfillment of both the spiritual and physical promises of the biblical covenants.[5] They do not see physical and national promises as inferior types that must be spiritualized or fulfilled non-literally. In this sense dispensationalists are more holistic in their understanding of God's kingdom purposes than many non-dispensationalists.

Three important beliefs of dispensationalism arise from the lists of Ryrie, Feinberg, and Blaising and Bock. First, these lists all mention the uniqueness of the church as a characteristic of dispensationalism. Though disagreement may exist on details of this distinction, dispensationalists are agreed that the church began at Pentecost (Acts 2) and is not to be identified

---

[4] Universal reconciliation does not mean universal salvation. Reconciliation also involves the judgment of the wicked (see Phil. 2:10–11).

[5] We acknowledge that more recent amillennialists like Anthony Hoekema have emphasized the fulfillment of physical blessings in the coming eternal state.

as Israel.[6] All dispensationalists reject "replacement theology" or "supersessionism" in which the church replaces or supersedes the nation Israel as the people of God.

Second, Ryrie, Feinberg, and Blaising and Bock point out that dispensationalists believe in a future for the nation Israel. Dispensationalists assert that Old Testament promises and covenants made with Israel will be fulfilled with the nation Israel in the future. Though dispensationalists may disagree as to how much the church also participates in the Old Testament promises and covenants, they are agreed that Israel will experience a future salvation and restoration. Israel as a nation must fulfill its role of leadership and service to other nations under the Messiah as passages like Isaiah 2:2–4 indicate.

Both Ryrie and Feinberg mention a third area—a dispensational approach to hermeneutics—as somehow being distinctive to dispensationalism. For Ryrie, dispensationalists interpret the Bible in a consistently literal manner while non-dispensationalists do not.[7] The issue is literal versus spiritual interpretation—dispensationalists interpret literally while non-dispensationalists, at times, interpret portions of Scripture non-literally.

Feinberg believes Ryrie was "too simplistic" in stating the matter this way.[8] According to Feinberg, the issue of hermeneutics "is not an easy issue," and he points out that many non-dispensational theologians claim to interpret the Bible literally. Their literalism, though, differs at points from the literal ap-

---

[6] According to Blaising and Bock, "One of the striking differences between progressive and earlier dispensationalists, is that progressives to do not view the church as an anthropological category in the same class as terms like Israel, Gentile Nations, Jews, and Gentile people. . . . The church is precisely redeemed humanity itself (both Jews and Gentiles) as it exists in this dispensation prior to the coming of Christ." *Progressive Dispensationalism*, 49.

[7] Charles C. Ryrie, *Dispensationalism* (Chicago: Moody, 1995), 84.

[8] Feinberg, "Systems of Discontinuity," 73.

proach of dispensationalists. Thus, for Feinberg, "The difference is not literalism v. non-literalism, but different understandings of what constitutes literal hermeneutics."[9]

According to Feinberg, the difference between dispensational and non-dispensational hermeneutics is found in three areas: (1) the relation of the progress of revelation to the priority of one Testament over the other; (2) the understanding and implications of the New Testament's use of the Old Testament; and (3) the understanding and implications of typology.[10] In sum, the main difference rests in how dispensationalists and non-dispensationalists view the relationship between the Old and New Testaments.

Feinberg's analysis appears more accurate, although I have found that non-dispensationalists sometimes use the terminology of "spiritualize" concerning the Old Testament. The main difference between dispensationalists and non-dispensationalists on the matter of hermeneutics is how each camp views the relationship between the testaments. As Herbert Bateman puts it, the central issue is "testament priority."[11] Testament priority is "a presuppositional preference of one testament over the other that determines a person's literal historical-grammatical hermeneutical starting point."[12]

An interpreter's testament priority assumptions are especially significant when interpreting how New Testament au-

---

[9] Feinberg, 74. Saucy makes the same point: "An analysis of non-dispensational systems, however, reveals that their less-than-literal approach to Israel in the Old Testament prophecies does not really arise from an *a priori* spiritualistic or metaphorical hermeneutic. Rather, it is the result of their interpretation of the New Testament using the same grammatico-historical hermeneutic as that of dispensationalists." Robert L. Saucy, *The Case for Progressive Dispensationalism: The Interface Between Dispensational & Non-dispensational Theology* (Grand Rapids: Zondervan, 1993), 20.

[10] Feinberg, 73–74.

[11] Herbert W. Bateman IV, "Dispensationalism Yesterday and Today," *Three Central Issues in Contemporary Dispensationalism: A Comparison of Traditional and Progressive Views*, ed. Herbert W. Bateman IV (Grand Rapids: Kregel, 1999), 38.

[12] Ibid.

thors use the Old Testament. Dispensationalists want to maintain a reference point in the Old Testament. They desire to give justice to the original authorial intent of the Old Testament writers in accord with historical-grammatical hermeneutics. Non-dispensationalists, on the other hand, emphasize the New Testament as their starting point for understanding the Old Testament. Feinberg explains the difference:

> Nondispensationalists begin with NT teaching as having priority and then go back to the OT. Dispensationalists often begin with the OT, but wherever they begin they demand that the OT be taken on its own terms rather than reinterpreted in the light of the NT.[13]

Thus, non-dispensationalists often start with the New Testament to understand Old Testament prophetic passages. The New Testament is the lens to view the Old Testament. This is what often leads to a 'non-literal' understanding of Old Testament texts since non-dispensationalists believe the New Testament sanctions less than literal understandings of Old Testament passages, especially prophetic texts about Israel. For example, note the following statements below from non-dispensational scholars.

In his defense of an amillennial view of the kingdom, Kim Riddlebarger asserted belief in *reinterpretation* of Old Testament eschatology:

> But eschatological themes are *reinterpreted* in the New Testament, where we are told these Old Testament images are

---

[13] Feinberg, 75. Feinberg's view is supported by the non-dispensationalist, George Ladd: "Here is the basic watershed between a dispensational and a non-dispensational theology. Dispensationalism forms its eschatology by a literal interpretation of the Old Testament and then fits the New Testament into it. A non-dispensational eschatology forms its theology from the explicit teaching of the New Testament." George Eldon Ladd, "Historic Premillennialism," *The Meaning of the Millennium: Four Views*, ed. Robert G. Clouse (Downers Grove: InterVarsity, 1977), 28.

types and shadows of the glorious realities that are fulfilled in Jesus Christ.[14]

Riddlebarger believes this priority of the NT over the OT means that at times the NT *spiritualizes* the OT prophecies:

> If the New Testament writers *spiritualize* Old Testament prophecies by *applying them in a nonliteral sense*, then the Old Testament passage must be seen in light of that New Testament interpretation, not vice versa.[15]

These quotes above reveal a close connection between belief in reinterpretation of the Old Testament and spiritualizing of the Old Testament. While referencing the kingdom, Louis Berkhof stated that Jesus "enlarged and *transformed* and *spiritualized* it."[16] Gary Burge argues that land promises of the OT have been "reinterpreted" in regard to Christ's kingdom:

> For as we shall see (and as commentators regularly show) while the land itself had a concrete application for most in Judaism, Jesus and his followers *reinterpreted* the promises that came to those in his kingdom.[17]

N. T. Wright uses "redefining" in regard to Jesus and His kingdom:

> Jesus spent His whole ministry *redefining* what the kingdom meant. He refused to give up the symbolic language of the

---

[14] Kim Riddlebarger, *A Case for Amillennialism*, 37. Emphases mine. For him, OT themes such as the nation of Israel, the temple, and the Davidic throne, are reinterpreted by the NT.

[15] Ibid. Emphases mine.

[16] Louis Berkhof, *The Kingdom of God* (Grand Rapids: Eerdmans, 1951), 13. Emphases mine.

[17] Gary M. Burge, *Jesus and the Land: The New Testament Challenge to "Holy Land" Theology* (Grand Rapids: Baker, 2010), 35. Emphasis mine.

kingdom, but filled it with such a new content that, as we have seen, he powerfully subverted Jewish expectations.[18]

As these examples show, for non-dispensationalists, the New Testament allegedly sanctions a non-literal understanding of some Old Testament passages, especially those regarding Israel. This occurs through reinterpretation and spiritualization. Dispensationalists do not believe this. They do not hold that God has to reinterpret or transcend His previous revelation. They affirm that the meaning of Old Testament passages lies in those passages and that the New Testament harmonizes with them and builds upon them. There is no need for one passage to have priority over others since all Scripture is inspired by God and makes its own contribution. All Bible passages complement and harmonize with each other, but no passage overrides the meaning of another passage. More on this issue will be covered in the section below.

Six Essential Beliefs of Dispensationalism

At this point, I offer six essential beliefs of dispensationalism. By "essential" I mean foundational beliefs that are central to dispensationalism, beliefs upon which the system stands or falls. These are also beliefs that if denied, would probably make one a non-dispensationalist. This list takes into consideration the offerings of Ryrie, Feinberg, and Blaising and Bock, but also offers my own contributions. These six essentials beliefs of dispensationalism are:

---

[18] N. T. Wright, *Jesus and the Victory of God*, (Minneapolis: Augsburg Fortress Press, 1997), 471. Emphasis mine. The above examples can also be found in my book, *He Will Reign Forever: A Biblical Theology of the Kingdom of God* (Silverton, OR: Lampion Press, 2017), 39–40.

1. The primary meaning of any Bible passage is found in that passage. The New Testament does not reinterpret or transcend Old Testament passages in a way that overrides or cancels the original authorial intent of the Old Testament writers.

This first point is a hermeneutical issue and is perhaps the most foundational of all the points. Dispensationalists affirm that the *starting point* for understanding all passages of Scripture, including those in the Old Testament, is the passages themselves, not other passages. This is what I referred to earlier as "passage priority." Thus, the primary meaning of Old Testament texts is found there. As progressive revelation unfolds later revelation complements and harmonizes with the older revelation, but it does not change previous Scripture.

This view is consistent with a high view of the New Testament. The New Testament at times adds additional information, offers commentary on, draws principles from, and shows how Christ fulfills the Mosaic Law. But the New Testament writers do not reinterpret or transcend the original intent of the Old Testament writers. The teachings and themes of the Old Testament are found in the New Testament without reinterpretation.

Thus, historical-grammatical hermeneutics should be used to understand the meaning of Old Testament passages. Paul D. Feinberg rightly stated, "The sense of any OT prediction must be determined through the application of historical-grammatical hermeneutics to that text."[19] Bruce A. Ware agrees and shows how this relates to Israel:

There can be no question that the prophets meant to communicate the promise of a national return of Israel to its land. To the extent that our hermeneutics are regulated by the principle of authorial intent, we are given ample reason

---

[19] Paul Feinberg, "Hermeneutics of Discontinuity," in *Continuity and Discontinuity*, 123.

to accept this literal rendering of what God, through the prophets, originally promised to his people Israel.[20]

For example, Hebrews 8:8–13, which quotes the original new covenant passage of Jeremiah 31:31–34, includes the church in the spiritual blessings of the new covenant, but since the new covenant was originally promised to Israel, the covenant must eventually involve national Israel. Paul makes this connection in Romans 11:26–27 when he quotes the new covenant passage of Isaiah 59 to support his claim that "all Israel" will be saved (see Isa. 59:20–21). Believing Gentiles experience salvation benefits of the new covenant in this age, but the New Testament does not exclude national Israel from the covenant. In fact, it speaks of national Israel's inclusion.

Thus, the new covenant has a "both/and" element to it— both Israel and the church. The church consisting of believing Jews and Gentiles in this age is related to the new covenant now (Heb. 8:8–13), and Israel will be related to the new covenant at the second coming of Christ (see Rom. 11:25–27). Bock states that, "The additional inclusion of some in the promise does not mean the original recipients are thereby excluded. *The expansion of promise need not mean the cancellation of earlier commitments God has made.* The realization of new covenant hope today for Gentiles does not mean that the promise made to Israel in Jeremiah 31 has been jettisoned."[21]

This approach is quite different from that of non-dispensationalists who often view the new covenant as being entirely fulfilled with the church in such a way that does not include national Israel. With this method the physical and material blessings of the new covenant allegedly find a spiritual or less

---

[20] Bruce A. Ware, "The New Covenant and the People(s) of God," in *Dispensationalism, Israel and the Church: The Search for Definition*, eds. Craig A. Blaising and Darrell L. Bock (Grand Rapids: Zondervan, 1992), 93.

[21] Blaising and Bock, *Progressive Dispensationalism*, 103–04. Emphasis in original.

literal fulfillment with the church who is now the new/true Israel in Christ.[22] Thus, one should not look for a future inclusion of national Israel into the covenant.

But this principle of maintaining the integrity of the original authorial intent of Old Testament texts has great importance to the eternal and unconditional covenants given to Israel in the Old Testament (Abrahamic, Davidic, New). John Feinberg has argued that God's unconditional covenants with Israel guarantee that the New Testament would not indicate these would not be fulfilled with Israel. God cannot contradict himself.

Feinberg also addresses this issue of the unconditional nature of certain promises for Israel and its implications for the concept of progressive revelation: "The crucial point is *how we know* whether something in the OT (especially prophecy about Israel's future) is still binding in the NT."[23] If an Old Testament promise is made unconditionally with a specific group such as Israel, then that promise must be fulfilled with that group. Progress of revelation cannot cancel unconditional promises to Israel:

> If an OT prophecy or promise is made unconditionally to a given people and is still unfulfilled to them even in the NT era, then the prophecy must still be fulfilled to them. While a prophecy given unconditionally to Israel has a fulfillment for the church if the NT *applies* it to the church, it

---

[22] The following people believe Hebrews 8:8–13 conveys the idea that the church now fully inherits the new covenant: Bruce K. Waltke, "Kingdom Promises as Spiritual," in *Continuity and Discontinuity*, 281; Wayne Grudem, *Systematic Theology: An Introduction to Biblical Doctrine* (Grand Rapids: Zondervan, 1994), 862; O. Palmer Robertson, *The Christ of the Covenants* (Phillipsburg, NJ: P&R, 1980), 289; Hans K. LaRondelle, *The Israel of God in Prophecy: Principles of Prophetic Interpretation* (Berrien Springs, MI: Andrews University Press, 1983), 116–118; John Bright, *The Kingdom of God: the Biblical Concept and Its Meaning for the Church* (Nashville: Abingdon, 1953), 228–29; Willem A. VanGemeren, "A Response," in *Dispensationalism, Israel and the Church: The Search for Definition*, eds. Craig A. Blaising and Darrell L. Bock (Grand Rapids: Zondervan, 1992), 337.

[23] John Feinberg, "Systems of Discontinuity," 76. Emphasis in original.

must also be fulfilled to Israel. Progress of revelation cannot cancel unconditional promises.[24]

David L. Turner rightly points out that "covenant theologians and dispensationalists disagree on the nature of progressive revelation."[25] He says, "Each group accuses the other of misinterpreting the NT due to alien presuppositions."[26] Turner then points out that dispensationalists deny that the New Testament reinterprets Old Testament promises to Israel: "It is their contention that the NT supplies no 'reinterpretation' of OT prophecy which would cancel the OT promises to Israel of a future historical kingdom. In their view the NT use of the OT does not radically modify the OT promises to Israel."[27]

This issue of what God revealed to the Old Testament authors is important. Turner claims that the non-dispensational understanding brings into question God's faithfulness to Israel: "If NT reinterpretation reverses, cancels, or seriously modifies OT promises to Israel, one wonders how to define the word 'progressive.' God's faithfulness to His promises to Israel must also be explained."[28]

Ryrie, too, points out that the New Testament does not contradict the meaning of Old Testament texts. He asserts, "New revelation cannot mean contradictory revelation. Later revelation on a subject does not make the earlier revelation mean something different."[29] "If this were so," according to Ryrie, "God would have to be conceived of as deceiving the Old Testament prophets when He revealed to them a nationalistic kingdom, since He would have known all the time that

---

Ibid. Emphasis in original.

25 David L. Turner, "The Continuity of Scripture and Eschatology: Key Hermeneutical Issues," *Grace Theological Journal* 6:2 (1985): 280.

26 Ibid., 280–81.

27 Ibid., 279.

28 Ibid., 281.

29 Ryrie, *Dispensationalism*, 84.

He would completely reverse the concept in later revelation."[30] For Ryrie, the concept of progressive revelation can be likened to a building in progress: "The superstructure does not replace the foundation."[31] Thus, the maintaining of the original authorial intent of Old Testaments passages is an essential of dispensationalism.

These quotations and points above show that dispensationalists take God's revelation in the Old Testament very seriously, and they are not apt to see Old Testament passages as reinterpreted or transcended. Thus, taking the Old Testament passages about Israel seriously is a foundational belief of dispensationalism.

2. Types exist but national Israel is not an inferior type that is superseded by the church.

Typology involves God-intended correspondences between Old Testament persons, places, things, events, and greater New Testament realities that correspond to these matters. For example, Adam is a type of Jesus (see Rom. 5:14; 1 Cor. 15:45). Also the Levitical priesthood of the Mosaic covenant was a type of Jesus' better new covenant priesthood (see Heb. 8–10). But how does the issue of typology relate to Israel and the church, and are dispensationalists blind to the existence of type connections in Scripture?

Non-dispensationalists often hold that the Old Testament as a whole is comprised of types and shadows of greater New Testament realities. In line with this idea, some assert that national Israel in the Old Testament functioned as a type of the

[30] Ibid. George N. H. Peters concurs, "If no restoration was intended; if all was to be understood typically, or spiritually, or conditionally, then surely the language was most eminently calculated to deceive the hearers. . . ." George N. H. Peters, *The Theocratic Kingdom of Our Lord Jesus, the Christ as Covenanted in the Old Testament*, vol. 2 (New York: Funk & Wagnalls, 1884; reprint, Grand Rapids: Kregel, 1988), 51.

[31] Ryrie, *Dispensationalism*, 84.

New Testament church. Supposedly, the people of God transforms from a national entity to a multi-ethnic spiritual entity that replaces or supersedes national Israel. Once Jesus arrived and the greater antitype, the church, was revealed, Israel's place as the people of God was allegedly transcended and superseded by the church.[32] For example, William E. Cox declared, "The historic Christian teaching holds that national Israel was a type or forerunner of the church, and that the church replaced Israel on the Day of Pentecost."[33] Mark W. Karlberg also claimed, "If one grants that national Israel in OT revelation was truly a type of the eternal kingdom of Christ, then it seems that, according to the canons of Biblical typology, national Israel can no longer retain any independent status whatever."[34] The founders of progressive covenantalism, Peter Gentry and Stephen Wellum, also argue against dispensationalism based on their understanding of typology:

> In the case of dispensational theology, if they viewed as typological both the land of Israel and the nation itself, then their view, at its core, would no longer be valid. Why? For the reason that the land promise would not require a future, "literal" fulfillment in the millennial age; the land itself is a type and pattern of Eden and thus the entire creation, which reaches its fulfillment in the dawning of a new creation. Christ, then, as the antitype of Israel, receives the land promise and fulfills it by his inauguration of a new covenant which is organically linked to the new creation.[35]

---

[32] See LaRondelle, *The Israel of God in Prophecy*, 45.

[33] William E. Cox, *Amillennialism Today*, 45–46. Get info

[34] Mark W. Karlberg, "The Significance of Israel in Biblical Typology," *Journal of the Evangelical Theological Society* 31:3 (1988): 259.

[35] Peter J. Gentry and Stephen J. Wellum, *Kingdom through Covenant: A Biblical-Theological Understanding of the Covenants* (Wheaton, IL.: Crossway, 2012), 122.

Dispensationalists, however, disagree with these understandings of how types and typology relate to Israel. Importantly, the issue here is not whether types exist or not. Dispensationalists believe in types, and it is not the case that if dispensationalists just opened their eyes to types and typology then they would see the error of their ways. Instead, dispensationalists take a different approach to understanding Israel and typology.

First, the people of Israel are a specific people who received specific national promises, so to use typology as a reason why they will not receive God's promises is not helpful. God keeps His promises to those whom the promises were made. In Jeremiah 31:35–37 God links Israel's perpetual existence as "a nation" with the sun, moon, stars, and foundations of the earth. With Romans 9:4–5 Paul explicitly affirms that the "covenants," "promises," and "temple service" still belong to national Israel, even when Israel as a whole was characterized by unbelief. The specific conditions and the people to whom the promises and covenants were originally made matter. God's integrity is tied to this. As Romans 11:28–29 declares:

> From the standpoint of the gospel they [Israel currently in unbelief] are enemies for your sake, but from the standpoint of God's choice they are beloved for the sake of the fathers; for the gifts and the calling of God are irrevocable.

God's electing purposes and calling of Israel are taken seriously by God. Thus, God's promises cannot simply be transferred to another without this impugning God's integrity. Paul said that when a covenant "has been ratified, no one sets it aside or adds conditions to it" (Gal. 3:15). One does not escape the problem by simply declaring the church is a "new Israel" who inherits the covenants to national Israel's exclusion. The same entity of national Israel that experienced curses for disobedience is the nation that will be restored (see Deut. 30 and Lev. 26). To claim that the church gets the promises but national Israel does not is like making wonderful promises to your son and then adopting another son and then giving the latter son the blessings you promised the first. That is not how fulfillment of promises works. Israel as a national entity received trans-generational national promises (see Deut. 30:1–10; Lev. 26:40–45), and with national Israel God will fulfill these promises. No theory of typology can overturn this.

Plus the salvation and restoration of Israel are reaffirmed in the New Testament (see Matt. 19:28; 23:39; Acts 1:6; 3:19–21; Rom. 11:26–27). If the New Testament reaffirms the hope of national Israel, this proves Israel does not lose theological significance, no matter what one's theory of typology is. If Israel is a transcended type, then why does the New Testament so often speak of national Israel's glorious future? We must be careful not to invent a theory of typology that overrides what clear and explicit passages concerning Israel are saying.

How does Jesus relate to Israel? Are there typological connections between Jesus and Israel? Dispensationalists believe there are typological connections between Jesus and national Israel. In Matthew 2 we see that events in Israel's history correspond to events in Jesus' life to reveal that Jesus is the ultimate Israelite who can restore national Israel (see Matt. 2:15/Hos. 11:1). Isaiah 49:1–6 predicted that Jesus' role as the true Servant of Israel allows Him to restore Israel and bring blessings to the Gentiles (Isa. 49:5–6). In regard to Jesus and Israel, typology exists to show corporate representation in which the Head (Jesus) restores the many (Israel) so the many can fulfill their mission of service to the nations and succeed where they once failed (see Isa. 2:2–4). So typological correspondences between Jesus and Israel affirm the restoration of national Israel, they do not make Israel non-significant nor do they redefine Israel.

Also, there are correspondences between Israel and the church in that both are called the people of God (1 Pet. 2:9–10). The Old Testament prophets predicted that believing Gentiles would become the people of God alongside believing

Israel, without becoming Israel (see Isa. 19:24–25). So the people of God expands to include Gentiles.

John Feinberg makes another helpful point that the nature of unconditional promises to Israel has implications for understanding Israel's relationship to typology:

> The unconditionality of the promises to Israel guarantees that the NT does not even implicitly remove those promises from Israel. OT civil and ceremonial laws and institutions are shadows and are explicitly removed in the NT. But unconditional promises are not shadows, nor are the peoples to whom they are given.[36]

Feinberg is right. If one rightly accepts that the people of Israel and the unconditional promises and covenants given to Israel are realities God takes seriously, then there is no need to view these as transcended types and shadows. Appealing to Hebrews 8–10 is no support for the supersessionist view of typology since the shadows in this section are matters related to the Mosaic Law. Unconditional promises are not shadows.

One of the problems with some typology theories of nondispensationalists is they create a story behind the story. Explicit passages seem to indicate that Israel, Israel's land, and promises (material and spiritual) to Israel all matter, but then we are told by theologians that these matters are not real. They are just types and shadows that lose significance. What makes this theory untenable is that it is not taught in the Bible, and the New Testament actually affirms the literal storyline begun in the Old Testament (see Matt. 19:28; Luke 1:32–33; 21:24; Acts 3:19–21; Rom. 9:4–5; 11:26–29).

So Paul Feinberg is correct that Israel is not viewed as a symbol or type of the church: "While historical-grammatical interpretation allows for symbols, types, and analogies, I see no

---

[36] John Feinberg, "Systems of Discontinuity," 76.

evidence that Israel is a symbol for the church, Palestine for the new Jerusalem, *et al.*"[37]

To summarize, dispensationalists are not saying there are no similarities between Israel and the church, but they insist that Israel is not a transcended type. Robert Saucy explains, "If a type is understood as shadow pointing forward to the reality of an antitype, then it is questionable whether Israel is a type."[38] On the other hand, if a type is viewed in terms of a correspondence between groups then a typological connection between Israel and the church may exist:

> If a type is defined as a general historical and theological correspondence, then the many analogies between Old Testament Israel and the New Testament people of God may well be explained by seeing Israel as a type of the church. But the correspondence with God's actions among Old Testament Israel would not in this understanding of typology deny the continued existence of that nation in the future.[39]

Thus, there may be a typological connection between Israel and the church, but this typological connection does not alter the original sense of the Old Testament promises to Israel. As David L. Turner explains, "Genuine typology and analogy between OT and NT should not be viewed as destructive to the literal fulfillment of the OT promises to Israel, but rather an indication of a greater continuity between Israel and the church."[40]

---

[37] Paul Feinberg, "Hermeneutics of Discontinuity," 124.

[38] Robert L. Saucy, *The Case for Progressive Dispensationalism: The Interface Between Dispensational & Non-dispensational Theology* (Grand Rapids: Zondervan, 1993), 32.

[39] Ibid., 31–32. See also W. Edward Glenny, "The Israelite Imagery of 1 Peter 2," in *Dispensationalism, Israel and the Church*, 180.

[40] Turner, "The Continuity of Scripture and Eschatology: Key Hermeneutical Issues," 282. See also Howard Taylor, "The Continuity of the People of God in Old and New Testaments," *Scottish Bulletin of Theology* 3 (1985): 14–15.

3. Israel and the church are distinct; thus, the church cannot be identified as the new and/or true Israel.

As the lists from Ryrie, Feinberg, and Blaising and Bock mentioned earlier indicate, all dispensationalists are united in denying the church is identified as the "new Israel." There may be differences among dispensationalists when it comes to the specifics of the relationship between the church and Israel or the exact relationship of the church to the biblical covenants, but all dispensationalists reject "replacement theology" or "supersessionism" in which the New Testament church is viewed as the replacement or fulfillment of the nation Israel as the people of God.[41] Jesus is coming again to rule nations and Israel will have a role in that worldwide reign (Isa. 2:2–4).

Traditional and progressive dispensationalists certainly have differences on how they view the church. Traditional dispensationalists tend to view the church as a distinct anthropological group that is different from both Israel and the nations. On the other hand, progressive dispensationalists tend to view the church as the soteriological or new covenant community of saved Jews and Gentiles in this age, starting with the events of Acts 2.[42] But both camps within dispensationalism agree that there is no biblical evidence to indicate the church is the new or true Israel that forever supersedes national Israel as the people of God.

Dispensationalists take seriously that believing Gentiles have been brought near to Israel and the covenants of Israel (see Eph. 2:11–22), but they also point out that the New Testament distinguishes Israel and the church in such a way that rules out the idea that the church is now identified as Israel or that the church entirely inherits Israel's promises and covenants to the exclusion of Israel.

---

[41] For a case against supersessionism from a dispensational perspective see Craig A. Blaising, "The Future of Israel as a Theological Question, *JETS* 44:3 (2001): 435–450.

[42] For more on this distinction see Blaising and Bock, *Progressive Dispensationalism*, 49–51.

Arnold Fruchtenbaum points out that "Israel" is used seventy-three times in the New Testament, but it is always used of ethnic Jews: "Of these seventy-three citations, the vast majority refer to national, ethnic Israel. A few refer specifically to Jewish believers who still are ethnic Jews."[43] Saucy confirms this point when he says, "The NT evidence reveals that outside of a few disputed references . . . the name Israel is related to the 'national' covenant people of the OT."[44] This is true even of the disputed "Israel of God" reference in Galatians 6:16. Some think Paul is calling the church the "Israel of God," but in this context in which Paul is refuting the gospel-threatening error of the Judaizers, Paul most probably singles out Christian Jews who have not fallen for the error of the Judaizers. Thus, the "Israel of God" refers to Jewish people who have believed in Jesus through faith.

For dispensationalists, it is also significant that the New Testament still consistently refers to the nation Israel as "Israel" even after the establishment of the church. Israel is addressed as a nation in contrast to Gentiles *after* the church was established at Pentecost (Acts 3:12; 4:8, 10; 5:21, 31, 35; 21:28). As Ryrie points out, "In Paul's prayer for natural Israel (Rom. 10:1) there is a clear reference to Israel as a national people distinct from and outside the church."[45] Ryrie argues that Paul's linking of national Israel to the covenants and promises of the Old Testament, even while in a state of unbelief, is further proof that the church has not entirely absorbed Israel's blessings:

> Paul, obviously referring to natural Israel as his 'kinsmen according to the flesh,' ascribes to them the covenants and the promises (Rom. 9:3–4). That these words were written

---

[43] Arnold G. Fruchtenbaum, "Israel and the Church," in *Issues in Dispensationalism*, eds. Wesley R. Willis and John R. Master (Chicago: Moody, 1994), 120.

[44] Robert L. Saucy, "Israel and the Church: A Case for Discontinuity," in *Continuity and Discontinuity*, 244–45.

[45] Ryrie, *Dispensationalism*, 127. Emphasis in original.

after the beginning of the church is proof that the church does not rob Israel of her blessings. The term *Israel* continues to be used for the natural (not spiritual) descendants of Abraham after the church was instituted, and it is not equated with the church.[46]

In addition, the book of Acts maintains a distinction between Israel and the church. Here both Israel and the church exist simultaneously but the term "Israel" is used twenty times and *ekklesia* (church) nineteen times. But the two groups are always kept distinct.[47] Thus, the continued use of the term "Israel" for the physical descendants of Jacob is evidence the church is not Israel. As Saucy explains, "The church is not . . . identified with 'Israel.' They share a similar identity as the people of God enjoying equally, the blessings of the promised eschatological salvation. But this commonality does not eliminate all distinctions between them."[48] In sum, the Israel/church distinction and the rejection of replacement theology continues to be a defining characteristic of dispensationalism.

4. Spiritual unity in salvation between Jews and Gentiles is compatible with a future functional role for Israel as a nation.

One argument against dispensationalism is that it does not do justice to the unity Jews and Gentiles experience in Christ. The emphasis on "one new man" (Eph. 2:15) and "one body" (Eph. 2:16) in the Bible is taken to mean there can be no future role for national Israel in a coming earthly kingdom since unity in Christ supposedly rules out any kind of special role for Israel. For example, in reference to Ephesians 2, Anthony

---

[46] Ibid. Emphasis in original.

[47] Fruchtenbaum, "Israel and the Church," 118. Emphases in original.

[48] Saucy, *The Case for Progressive Dispensationalism*, 210. For Saucy "It is the lack of national characteristics that distinguishes the church from Israel" (210).

Hoekema declares, "All thought of a separate purpose for believing Jews is here excluded."[49] In regard to Ephesians 2:11–15, Raymond Zorn argues, "Through Christ's fulfilling of the law an end has come to the exclusivity of Israel as a holy nation and a holy people."[50] Wayne Grudem says that Ephesians 2 "gives no indication of any distinctive plan for Jewish people ever to be saved apart from inclusion in the one body of Christ, the church."[51] For non-dispensationalists, it appears unlikely that God would bring Jews and Gentiles together only to make a distinction between the two groups in the future. To do so appears to be going backward. As Hoekema declares, it is like putting the scaffolding back on a finished building:

> To suggest that God has in mind a separate future for Israel, in distinction from the future he has planned for Gentiles, actually goes contrary to God's purpose. It is like putting the scaffolding back up after the building has been finished. It is like turning the clock of history back to Old Testament times. It is imposing Old Testament separateness upon the New Testament, and ignoring the progress of revelation.[52]

But dispensationalists hold that spiritual unity between believing Jews and Gentiles in Jesus does not cancel God-ordained functional distinctions between Jews and Gentiles in the coming kingdom of Jesus. Both groups are saved the same way—by grace alone, through faith alone, in Christ alone. In this sense there is no distinction between Jew and Gentile. However, salvific unity between Jews and Gentiles does not erase ethnic or functional distinctions between the two groups. As Carl Hoch states:

---

[49] Anthony A. Hoekema, *The Bible and the Future* (Grand Rapids: Eerdmans, 1979), 200.

[50] Zorn, *Christ Triumphant*, 190.

[51] Grudem, *Systematic Theology*, 862.

[52] Hoekema, *The Bible and the Future*, 201.

Paul's comments in Ephesians, however, exclude any salvific priority for Israel in the ecclesiological structure of the new man. . . . However, while there is no longer *salvific* advantage, there is still an *ethnic* distinction between Jews and Gentiles. Paul continues to speak of Jews and Gentiles as distinct ethnic groups in his letters (Rom. 1:16; 9:24; 1 Cor. 1:24; 12:13; Gal. 2:14, 15).[53]

This understanding that salvific equality does not rule out functional distinctions is seen in other examples in Scripture. For example, according to Galatians 3:28 men and women share equally in salvation blessings but the Bible still teaches that men and women have different roles (see 1 Tim. 2:9–15). Thus, in the case of men and women, salvific unity does not nullify functional distinctions. The same is true for elders and non-elders in a church. Both are equal in essence and share the same spiritual blessings, but elders have a distinct role in the plan of God (see Heb. 13:17). The same distinction could be made between parents and children or even the Trinity itself in which there is equality of essence among the three members of the Godhead yet functional distinctions within this oneness. The Father, Son, and Holy Spirit are all God, yet they are distinct in person and function. Thus, equality in essence and spiritual blessings does not nullify all distinctions. As Saucy writes:

> The union of Jew and Gentile in the church does not rule out the possibility of *functional* distinctions between Israel and the other nations in the future—in the same way that there are functional distinctions among believers in the church today amid spiritual equality.[54]

---

[53] Carl B. Hoch, Jr., "The New Man of Ephesians 2," in *Dispensationalism, Israel and the Church*, 118. Emphases in original.

[54] Saucy, *The Case for Progressive Dispensationalism*, 167. Emphasis in original.

Saucy brings up a good point in noting that functional distinctions for Israel are related to the future and not the present. It is only when God saves and restores national Israel and Jesus begins to rule the nations at His second coming (see Rev. 19:15) that Israel will have a special role of leadership and service to the nations that also are the people of God (see Amos 9:11–12).

Dispensationalists recognize that God's creation evidences the wonder and beauty of both unity and diversity. Not only does unity and diversity describe the Trinity this paradigm is true of many things in God's world. And this extends to the people(s) of God. Thus, when it comes to the issue of salvific unity between believing Jews and Gentiles *and* a future role of Israel to the nations in a millennial kingdom, the dispensationalist says, "Yes, it is a both/and situation."

5. The nation Israel will be both saved and restored with a unique functional role in a future earthly millennial kingdom.

This point has not often been clarified well by dispensationalists, but it is important.[55] Often dispensationalists state that belief in "a future for Israel" or "the salvation of Israel" is a distinguishing characteristic of dispensationalism. But these statements are not specific enough. Some non-dispensationalists also affirm the above two statements. In fact, a fair number of non-dispensationalists, including many postmillennialists and some amillennialists, believe in a literal salvation of many ethnic Israelites based on Paul's words in Romans 11:26 that "all Israel will be saved." This view was held by many of the theologians of the Patristic Era. More recently, this understanding of Romans 11:26 has been promoted by Handley C. G. Moule, John Murray, Leon Morris, F. F. Bruce, and Wayne

---

[55] Arnold Fruchtenbaum would be one notable exception.

Grudem.[56] So it is not enough to claim belief in a future salvation of Israel is only a dispensational view. What distinguishes all dispensationalists, however, is belief in a *restoration* of Israel. The concept of restoration certainly includes the idea of salvation for Israel, but it goes beyond that. "Restoration" involves the idea of Israel being reinstalled as a nation, in her land, with a specific identity and role of service to the nations. In a literal, earthly kingdom—a millennium—the nation Israel will serve a functional role to the nations (Isa. 2:2–4). This point is something all dispensationalists affirm while non-dispensationalists often deny. Even some historic premillennialists who agree with dispensationalists on the issues of a national salvation of Israel and a future millennial kingdom disagree concerning whether Israel will be restored with a unique identity and function that is distinct from the church.

Thus, there is a difference between saying Israel will be saved into the church, and saying the nation Israel will saved and restored with a unique identity and role to other nations in an earthly millennium. Dispensationalists affirm the latter.

This view does not occur in a vacuum. Part of the reason for a restoration of national Israel is because Jesus the Messiah is going to rule over literal nations at His return (Rev. 19:15). Zechariah 14 explicitly states that when the Lord returns to earth He is going to rule over nations, Egypt being explicitly named (Zech. 14:9, 18–19; Isa. 19:24–25). This salvation and restoration of national Israel is also consistent with Jesus' identity and role as the true and ultimate Israelite. According to Isaiah 49:3–6 Jesus is the ultimate Servant of Israel who restores the nation Israel and brings blessings to Gentiles. Many

---

[56] Handley C. G. Moule, *The Epistle of St. Paul to the Romans* (New York: A. C. Armstrong & Son, 1899), 311–12; John Murray, *The Epistle to the Romans*, vol. 2 (Grand Rapids: Eerdmans, 1997), 99; Leon Morris, *The Epistle to the Romans* (Grand Rapids: Eerdmans, 1988), 421; F. F. Bruce, *The Letter of Paul to the Romans: An Introduction and Commentary*, TNTC, vol. 6 (Grand Rapids: Eerdmans, 1985; reprint, 1990), 209; Wayne Grudem, *Systematic Theology: An Introduction to Biblical Doctrine* (Grand Rapids: Zondervan, 1994), 861, n. 17.

non-dispensationalists think Jesus' identity as true Israel means the end of national Israel's significance in God's purposes, but the opposite is the case. Jesus is the corporate head of Israel who saves and restores the nation Israel.

6. There are multiple senses of "seed of Abraham," thus the church's identification as "seed of Abraham" does not cancel God's promises to the believing Jewish "seed of Abraham."

Galatians 3:7 states that those who exercise faith are "sons of Abraham." Galatians 3:29 also declares that those who belong to Christ are "Abraham's descendants" and "heirs according to promise." Some non-dispensationalists have argued that since Gentiles are "sons" and "descendants" (or "seed") of Abraham they must also be spiritual Jews.[57] Dispensationalists, however, have contested this understanding. They have done so by challenging the idea that being a "son" or "seed" of Abraham automatically makes one a Jew. Saucy, for example, asserts that Abraham's fatherhood goes beyond being the father of ethnic Israel since the patriarch trusted God before he was circumcised:

> If Abraham were merely the father of Israel, we would have to conclude that the Gentiles who are now a part of this seed are therefore a part of Israel. But according to the New Testament, Abraham is more than that; he is portrayed as the father of both the people of Israel and of the Gentiles. On the grounds that Abraham was a believer be-

---

[57] The following authors assert that Galatians 3:7, 29 teaches that believing Gentiles are considered spiritual Jews: Ladd, "Historic Premillennialism," 24; Hoekema, *The Bible and the Future*, 198–99; William Neil, *The Letter of Paul to the Galatians* (Cambridge: Cambridge University Press, 1967), 62; Strimple, "Amillennialism," 88–89; LaRondelle, *The Israel of God in Prophecy*, 108; Bright, *The Kingdom of God*, 227; Bruce K. Waltke, "Kingdom Promises as Spiritual," in *Continuity and Discontinuity*, 267.

fore he was circumcised—that is, before he was recognized as a Hebrew—the Apostle Paul declared him to be "the father of all who believe but have not been circumcised . . . and . . . also the father of the circumcised" (Ro 4:9–12; cf. v. 16).[58]

The Abrahamic covenant from its initial giving was intended to involve the great nation of Israel and the Gentile groups of the world (Gen. 12:2–3; 22:18). Thus, the intent of the Abrahamic covenant was to bless the Gentiles through Abraham and Israel. Its goal was never to make believing Gentiles part of Israel. As Saucy mentioned, Romans 4:9–12 states that Abraham expressed saving faith before he was circumcised. This qualifies him to be the father of two groups—Gentiles who believe and Jews who believe. But this does not mean believing Gentiles become Israel in any sense. Thus a proper "seed" theology does not rule out God's purposes for Israel. "The fact that the true seed of Abraham includes both Jews and Gentiles does not rule out a continuing distinction for Israel in the New Testament. Nor should the calling of the Gentiles as the seed of Abraham be construed as the formation of a 'new spiritual Israel' that supersedes the Old Testament nation of Israel."[59]

Dispensationalists point out that the concept of "seed of Abraham" is used in several different ways in the New Testament, and that context determines which meaning is in mind. Fruchtenbaum, for example, lists four senses of "seed of Abraham." First, he says it can refer to those who are biological descendants of Abraham.[60] Second, it can refer to the Messiah, who is the unique individual seed of Abraham (Gal. 3:16).[61] Third, Fruchtenbaum says it can refer to the righteous remnant

[58] Saucy, *The Case for Progressive Dispensationalism*, 50.

[59] Ibid.

[60] See Fruchtenbaum, *Israelology*, 702.

[61] See Ibid.

of Israel (cf. Isa 41:8 with Rom 9:6).[62] Fourth, it can be used in a spiritual sense for believing Jews and Gentiles (Gal. 3:29).[63] It is in this last sense—the spiritual sense—that believing Gentiles are the seed of Abraham. John Feinberg also distinguishes between a physical sense and a spiritual sense of being a seed of Abraham. According to him, non-supersessionists hold that "no sense (spiritual especially) is more important than any other, and that no sense cancels out the meaning and implications of the other senses."[64] Thus, the application of the titles "sons of Abraham" or "seed of Abraham" to believing Gentiles does not mean that believing Gentiles are spiritual Jews or part of Israel.[65]

Together, these six points mentioned above comprise the foundation of dispensational theology. These six points best show what dispensationalism as a system is about.

---

[62] See Ibid.

[63] See Ibid.

[64] John Feinberg, "Systems of Discontinuity," 73.

[65] Fruchtenbaum states, "What replacement theologians need to prove their case is a statement in Scripture that all believers are of 'the seed of Jacob.' Such teaching would indicate that the church is spiritual Israel or that Gentile Christians are spiritual Jews." Fruchtenbaum, "Israel and the Church," in *Issues in Dispensationalism* (Chicago: Moody, 1994), 126–27.

3

Myths about Dispensationalism

We have discussed the essential beliefs of dispensationalism. At this point we shift to examining issues that are often thought to be essential to dispensationalism but really are not. Throughout its history, dispensationalism has been linked with various views that are not foundational to this theology. This has been especially true in regard to issues related to the doctrine of salvation but includes other areas as well. But these claims show a lack of understanding of the true nature of dispensationalism.

Not every theological system has an inherent relationship to every area of Christian theology. For example, reformed theology has specific views on the doctrines of Scripture, God's sovereignty, and salvation. But reformed theology does not lead to any specific view of eschatology or the millennium. There are reformed theologians who are amillennialists, postmillennialists, and premillennialists. To attempt to link reformed theology to a specific millennial view would be incorrect since it is not inherently related to the millennial issue.

The same is true for dispensationalism. This theology is inherently linked to certain areas of theology but is not inherently linked to others. Dispensationalism is primarily concerned with the doctrines ecclesiology (church) and eschatology (end times). But it does not promote a specific soteriological view. Again, this does not mean dispensationalists are not concerned about the doctrine of salvation. Dispensationalists affirm that salvation is based on grace alone through faith alone in Christ alone. In this there is agreement. But when it comes to variations on other issues related to soteriology, particularly concerning Calvinism and Arminianism, this is not an emphasis of dispensationalism. As John Feinberg writes:

> Dispensationalism becomes very important in regard to ecclesiology and eschatology, but is really not about those other areas. Some think salvation is at the heart of Dispensationalism, because they erroneously think Dispensationalism teaches multiple methods of salvation. Those who properly understand the position realize that its emphasis lies elsewhere.[1]

John MacArthur, a dispensationalist who has been heavily involved in soteriological debates with other dispensationalists, also rightly asserts that eschatology and ecclesiology, not soteriology, are at the heart of dispensationalism:

> So dispensationalism shapes one's *eschatology* and *ecclesiology*. That is the extent of it. Pure dispensationalism has no ramifications for the doctrines of God, man, sin, or sanctification. More significantly, true dispensationalism makes no relevant contribution to *soteriology*, or the doctrine of salvation.[2]

The conclusions of Feinberg and MacArthur are consistent with the words of the non-dispensationalist, O.T. Allis, who said, "The primary features of this movement [dispensationalism] were two in number. The one related to the Church. . . . The other had to do with prophecy."[3]

---

[1] John S. Feinberg, "Systems of Discontinuity," *Continuity and Discontinuity: Perspectives on the Relationship Between the Old and New Testaments*, ed. John S. Feinberg (Wheaton, IL: Crossway, 1988), 70–71.

[2] John F. MacArthur, Jr., *Faith Works: The Gospel According to the Apostles* (Dallas: Word, 1993), 222.

[3] Oswald T. Allis, *Prophecy and the Church* (Philadelphia: Presbyterian and Reformed, 1945), 9. Klooster, when addressing dispensationalism's views on law and

Our assertion that dispensationalism is primarily about ecclesiology and eschatology and not soteriology is also evidenced in the works of leading dispensationalists who have addressed what dispensationalism is about. When one surveys these works, it becomes evident that dispensationalism does not promote a particular soteriological view.

For example, Ryrie's *Dispensationalism Today* devoted a chapter to "Salvation," but the chapter was mostly a refutation of the charge that dispensationalism taught multiple ways of salvation. He does not argue that dispensationalism inherently leads to any particular soteriological view. In his 1993 work, *The Case for Progressive Dispensationalism*, Robert L. Saucy discussed ecclesiological, eschatological, and hermeneutical issues related to dispensationalism, but he promoted no particular dispensational soteriology.[4] In a 1992 book edited by Blaising and Bock called *Dispensationalism, Israel and the Church: The Search for Definition*, dispensational authors wrote on various ecclesiological, eschatological, and hermeneutical issues, but none argued for a certain dispensational soteriology.[5] The same is true for Blaising and Bock's 1993 book, *Progressive Dispensationalism*.[6] Except for addressing misconceptions about dispensational views on law and grace, there was no direct discussion of any dispensational soteriology. Paul Enns, a dispensationalist, devoted a chapter to "Dispensational Theology" in his 1989

---

grace, Israel and the church, and the covenants, states, "All of this bears on significant differences in eschatology." Fred H. Klooster, "The Biblical Method of Salvation: A Case for Continuity," *Continuity and Discontinuity*, 133–34. According to Richard, "The distinction between Soteriology and ecclesiology as major segments of systematic theology allows dispensationalism to be separated from the soteriological systems (Calvinism, Arminianism, etc.)." Ramesh P. Richard, "Soteriological Inclusivism and Dispensationalism," *Bibliotheca Sacra*, 151/601 (January-March 1994): 97, n. 44.

[4] Robert L. Saucy, *The Case for Progressive Dispensationalism: The Interface Between Dispensational & Non-dispensational Theology* (Grand Rapids: Zondervan, 1993).

[5] Craig A. Blaising and Darrell L. Bock, eds. *Dispensationalism, Israel and the Church: The Search for Definition* (Grand Rapids: Zondervan, 1992).

[6] Craig A. Blaising and Darrell L. Bock, *Progressive Dispensationalism: An Up-To-Date Handbook of Contemporary Dispensational Thought* (Wheaton, IL: Bridgepoint, 1993).

book, *The Moody Handbook of Theology*.[7] He offered one paragraph to the issue of salvation. The thrust of the paragraph, though, was to refute the argument that dispensationalism taught multiple ways of salvation. No specific dispensational soteriology was mentioned.

These works by leading dispensationalists are important because they reveal what is at the heart of dispensationalism. It is significant that none of these works connects dispensationalism to a certain soteriological perspective.

Of course, I am not asserting dispensationalists do not hold certain soteriological views, of course they do. A distinction, though, must be made between what individual dispensationalists hold to and what dispensationalism as a system is based upon. Not heeding this distinction is the fundamental error of those who link dispensationalism with certain soteriological views. They are, as Feinberg puts it, "reacting to what they think dispensationalists hold rather than to the logic of the system itself."[8] Now let us look at common myths about dispensationalism.

Myth 1: Dispensationalism Teaches Multiple Ways of Salvation

According to Ryrie, the "the most frequently heard objection against dispensationalism is that it supposedly teaches several ways of salvation."[9] John Wick Bowman made this accusation in 1956 when he said that dispensationalists are "clearly left with two methods of salvation."[10] In 1960, Clarence Bass argued that dispensational distinctions between law and grace and Israel and the church "inevitably result in a multiple form

---

[7] Paul Enns, *The Moody Handbook of Theology* (Chicago: Moody, 1989).

[8] John S. Feinberg, "Salvation in the Old Testament," *Tradition and Testament: Essays in Honor of Charles Lee Feinberg*, eds. John S. Feinberg and Paul D. Feinberg (Chicago: Moody, 1981), 48.

[9] Charles C. Ryrie, *Dispensationalism* (Chicago: Moody, 1995), 105.

[10] See John Wick Bowman, "The Bible and Modern Religions II, Dispensationalism," *Interpretation* 10 (April 1956), 178.

of salvation—that men are not saved the same way in all ages."[11] As will be shown this claim is false. Much of the debate centered on a note concerning John 1:17 in the 1909 *Scofield Reference Bible*:

> As a dispensation grace begins with the death and resurrection of Christ (Rom. 3:24–26; 4:24, 25). The point of testing is no longer legal obedience as the condition of salvation, but acceptance or rejection of Christ, with good works as the fruit of salvation.[12]

Some saw in this statement an explicit assertion that Scofield and dispensationalists believed in multiple ways of salvation.[13] Scofield's views in the *Scofield Reference Bible* were often equated with dispensationalism since he was viewed as the leading dispensationalist of his era. According to Klooster, the perception that dispensationalism taught multiple ways of salvation was commonly held by non-dispensationalists until 1965.[14] At this time, Ryrie published his work *Dispensationalism Today* in which he responded to the charge that dispensationalism taught multiple ways of salvation.[15] Ryrie asserted that earlier dispensationalists, including Scofield, did not teach multiple ways of salvation. They made "unguarded statements that would have been more carefully worded if they were being made in the light of today's debate."[16]

---

[11] Clarence B. Bass, *Backgrounds to Dispensationalism* (Grand Rapids: Eerdmans, 1960), 34. See also J. Barton Payne, *The Imminent Appearing of Christ* (Grand Rapids: Eerdmans, 1962), 31–32.

[12] *Scofield Reference Bible* (New York: Oxford, 1909), 1115, n 1(2).

[13] See William E. Cox, *Why I Left Scofieldism* (Phillipsburg: Presbyterian and Reformed, n.d.), 19.

[14] Fred Klooster, "The Biblical Method of Salvation: Continuity," in *Continuity and Discontinuity*, 132.

[15] Charles C. Ryrie, *Dispensationalism Today* (Chicago: Moody, 1965), 110–31.

[16] Ibid., 106–07.

Ryrie also called on non-dispensationalists to acknowledge the significant change in the *New Scofield Reference Bible* regarding John 1:17 in which the controversial wording was removed and a clear statement of one way of salvation was affirmed. The note now reads:

> Under the former dispensation, law was shown to be powerless to secure righteousness and life for a sinful race (Gal. 3:21–22). Prior to the cross man's salvation was through faith (Gen. 15:6; Rom. 4:3), being grounded on Christ's atoning sacrifice, viewed anticipatively by God; now it is clearly revealed that salvation and righteousness are received by faith in the crucified and resurrected Savior.[17]

Since the publishing of *Dispensationalism Today*, other dispensationalists have joined Ryrie in bringing clarity to this issue. As Saucy writes, "While it cannot be denied that there is some unresolved tension in these earlier statements, dispensationalists have more recently been careful to explain that the progression in the dispensations involves no change in the fundamental principle of salvation by grace."[18]

As a result of Ryrie's work, the writings of other dispensationalists, and the *New Scofield Reference Bible* revision, some non-dispensationalists became convinced that dispensationalism does not teach multiple ways of salvation. Fred H. Klooster is one example:

> In light of this significant revision in the *New Scofield Reference Bible* and the arguments of such dispensationalists as Ryrie and [John] Feinberg, the old charge should be dropped. One must proceed from the acknowledgement

---

[17] *The New Scofield Reference Bible*, editorial committee, E. Schuyler English et al. (New York: Oxford, 1967), 1124, n1(2).

[18] Saucy, *The Case For Progressive Dispensationalism*, 14.

that Dispensationalism recognizes a single way of salvation throughout the Scripture. Salvation is now and has always been by grace alone—*sola gratia*! This agreement is a cause for joy; its acknowledgment should not be made grudgingly.[19]

Klooster's perspective is also shared by Anthony Hoekema: "We gratefully acknowledge their [dispensationalists'] insistence that in every age salvation is only through grace, on the basis of the merits of Christ."[20] Taking into account the *New Scofield Reference Bible* and Ryrie's *Dispensationalism Today*, Daniel Fuller wrote, "In comparing these contemporary statements of dispensationalism with covenant theology, we conclude that there is no longer any substantive difference between the two on the subject of the law and the gospel."[21]

Klooster, Hoekema, and Fuller showed integrity by evaluating this issue objectively. Sadly, not all critics of dispensationalism followed their lead. In his 1991 book, *Wrongly Dividing the Word of Truth: A Critique of Dispensationalism,* John Gerstner accused all dispensationalists of teaching more than one way of salvation. He said, "We must sadly accuse dispensationalists (of all varieties) of teaching, always implicitly and sometimes explicitly, that there is more than one way of salvation and, in the process of developing that theology, excluding the one and only way even from this dispensation of grace."[22] In the 2015

---

[19] Klooster, "The Biblical Method of Salvation: Continuity," 133. Klooster even asserted that there is "significant evangelical agreement" between dispensationalists and Reformed theologians on the issue of "a single way of salvation," 133.

[20] Anthony A. Hoekema, *The Bible and the Future* (Grand Rapids: Eerdmans, 1979), 194.

[21] Daniel Fuller, *Gospel and Law: Contrast or Continuum?* (Grand Rapids: Eerdmans, 1980), 45. Erickson writes, "Some critics of dispensationalism have imputed to its supporters a belief in new ways or channels of salvation. More correctly, however, dispensationalists say that while new light has been shed upon the relationship between God and man, no new way of entering into that relationship has ever been insinuated." Millard J. Erickson, *A Basic Guide to Eschatology: Making Sense of the Millennium* (Grand Rapids: Baker, 1998), 110.

[22] John H. Gerstner, *Wrongly Dividing the Word of Truth: A Critique of Dispensationalism* (Brentwood, TN: Wolgemuth & Hyatt, 1991), 168.

book, *Perspectives on Israel and the Church: 4 Views*, covenant theologian, Robert Reymond, claimed dispensationalists teach
"different 'plans of salvation.'"[23] In the same book, adherents
of progressive covenantalism, Chad O. Brand and Tom Pratt,
Jr., said, "The dispensational approach virtually requires multiple pathways to this salvation."[24]

So the old discredited charge against dispensationalism
continues. But contrary to the claims of these men the evidence indicates dispensationalism does not teach multiple ways
of salvation. No credible dispensational theologian or school
teaches this. And even if some dispensationalist somewhere
were found who did affirm this, it certainly is not normative or
required by the dispensational system. As John Feinberg
pointed out, there is nothing inherent within dispensationalism
that leads dispensationalists to conclude that the Bible teaches
multiple ways of salvation:

> Thus, the question of whether dispensationalism necessi-
> tates a multiple methods of salvation view, or a single way
> of salvation position is irrelevant. Soteriology is not the
> determinative area for Dispensationalism.[25]

---

[23] Robert L. Reymond, "The Traditional Covenantal View," in *Perspectives on
Israel and the Church: 4 Views*, ed. Chad O. Brand (Nashville, TN: B&H, 2015), 25.

[24] Chad O. Brand and Tom Pratt Jr., "The Progressive Covenantal View," in
Perspectives on Israel and the Church: 4 Views, 236.

[25] Feinberg, "Tradition and Testament," 48. It is not correct, as Gerstner and
some older non-dispensationalists have asserted, that the dispensational distinctions
between Israel and the church naturally lead to multiple ways of salvation. Distinctions between groups can exist without different methods of salvation being present. No evidence exists that any leading dispensational theologians ever taught that
the Israel/church distinctions included the idea of different methods of salvation
for the two groups.

Myth 2: Dispensationalism Is Inherently Tied to Arminianism

A second erroneous charge often made against dispensationalism is that it teaches or inherently leads to Arminianism.[26] Thus, dispensationalism at its core is allegedly opposed to Calvinism. For example, according to Keith A. Mathison, "Dispensationalism has adopted a semi-Pelagian, Arminian doctrine not based on Scripture."[27] Gerstner, too, viewed dispensationalism as inherently "anti-Calvinistic" and accused dispensationalism of denying all five points of Calvinism.[28] He also says, "In its views of the creation of man, the Fall, the Atonement, soteriology, and eschatology, this system is a variation of the Arminian system."[29] J. I. Packer appeared impressed with Gerstner's assertions when he stated, "He [Gerstner] sets out to show that Calvinism and Dispensationalism are radically opposed, and he proves his point."[30]

Mathison and Gerstner point to Arminian-like statements from dispensationalists that supposedly link dispensationalism with Arminianism. And in some cases, they are correct that some dispensationalists hold Arminian views. But many dispensationalists do not. The real issue is whether dispensationalism is inherently connected with Arminianism. Our assertion is that it is not. We offer three reasons for our claim.

---

[26] Arminianism takes its name from Jacobus Arminius (1560–1609) and the movement that followed his teachings. Arminianism is known for the following views: conditional election is based on the foreknowledge of God; God's grace can be resisted; Christ's atonement was universal in scope; man has a free will—through prevenient grace he can cooperate with God; and man can lose his salvation through disobedience. Arminianism was condemned by the Synod of Dort in 1619.

[27] Keith A. Mathison, *Dispensationalism: Rightly Dividing the People of God?* (Phillipsburg: P&R, 1995), 50–51.

[28] Gerstner, 115.

[29] Ibid.

[30] Gerstner, *Wrongly Dividing the Word of Truth* with an endorsement by J. I. Packer, back cover.

First, as already indicated, dispensationalism is primarily about ecclesiology, eschatology, and hermeneutics, not soteriology. In addressing whether dispensationalism is related to the Arminianism/Calvinism issue, John Feinberg explains why it is not:

> Neither Calvinism nor Arminianism is at the essence of Dispensationalism. . . . This matter is not at the essence of Dispensationalism, because Calvinism and Arminianism are very important in regard to the concepts of God, man, sin, and salvation. Dispensationalism becomes very important in regard to ecclesiology and eschatology, but is really not about those other areas.[31]

Second, although some dispensationalists have Arminian tendencies, there are also dispensationalists who are Calvinists—even five-point Calvinists. As David L. Turner explains, "There are certain dispensationalists, myself included, who hold Calvinistic theology, including limited atonement."[32] In addition, to Turner, the late S. Lewis Johnson, Jr. was another dispensationalist who held to all five points of Calvinism.[33] Jeffrey Khoo points out that James Oliver Buswell (1895–1977) was a "dispensational premillennialist" who was also "a true and consistent reformed scholar. . . a five-point (TULIP) Calvinist."[34] Buswell, a member of the Bible Presbyterian Church, was "perhaps the most prominent reformed scholar who took

---

[31] Feinberg, "Systems of Discontinuity," 70.

[32] Turner, David L. "'Dubious Evangelicalism'? A Response to John Gerstner's Critique of Dispensationalism," *Grace Theological Journal*, 12/2 (Fall 1991): 268.

[33] S. Lewis Johnson, Jr., "The Testimony of John to Jesus," *Believers Bible Bulletin*, (December 20, 1981), 3.

[34] Jeffrey Khoo, "Dispensational Premillennialism in Reformed Theology: The Contribution of J. O. Buswell to the Millennial Debate," *Journal of the Evangelical Theological Society* 44.4 (January 2001): 714.

a dispensational premillennial view."[35] Plus many of the early dispensationalists were Presbyterians.

Both Mathison and Gerstner deny a connection between dispensationalism and Calvinism, but they do not logically show why. Nor do they explain why dispensational theologians like Turner, Johnson, and Buswell cannot be Calvinists. Instead of just quoting certain Arminian dispensationalists, the arguments of Gerstner and Mathison would be more impressive if they could logically show why dispensationalism is inherently anti-Calvinistic and why dispensationalists who claim to be Calvinists are not really Calvinists. There is, however, no logical reason why a dispensationalist cannot be a Calvinist. As Richard Mayhue observes, "One may be a five-point Calvinist and still be a consistent dispensationalist."[36]

Finally, some non-dispensational scholars have actually documented a close historical connection between dispensationalism and Calvinism. According to Vern Poythress, "Scofield's teachings and notes are evangelical. They are mildly Calvinistic in that they maintain a high view of God's sovereignty."[37] Church historian George M. Marsden says, "Dispensationalism was essentially Reformed in its nineteenth-century origins and had in later nineteenth-century America spread most among revival-oriented Calvinists."[38] C. Norman Kraus

---

[35] Ibid., 698. Khoo himself is a dispensationalist who is also Reformed: "As a Bible-Presbyterian minister, I am Reformed and hold to the covenant system of theology. In the area of eschatology, I hold to a premillennial view that sees a distinction between Israel as God's chosen nation and the Church as the spiritual body of Christ. As regards the rapture, I take the pretribulational view." Khoo, 716.

[36] Richard L. Mayhue, "Who Is Wrong? A Review of John Gerstner's *Wrongly Dividing The Word of Truth*," *Masters Seminary Journal*, 3/1 (Spring 1992), 89.

[37] Vern S. Poythress, *Understanding Dispensationalists*, 2d ed. (Phillipsburg: P & R, 1994), 20.

[38] George M. Marsden, "Introduction: Reformed and American," *Reformed Theology in America: A History of Its Modern Development*, 2d ed., George M. Marsden, ed. (Grand Rapids: Baker, 1997), 8.

declares that "the basic theological affinities of dispensationalism are Calvinistic."[39] In his discussion of Arminianism and reformed theology, Wayne Grudem says, "Both views are found among . . . Dispensationalists."[40]

I highlight the findings of these scholars not to prove that dispensationalism is inherently Calvinistic but to show that if one wants to press the issue, it can be argued that dispensationalism has a closer historical connection to Calvinism than to Arminianism. Thus, the claim that dispensationalism is inherently connected to Arminianism is false and should be dropped. It is a myth.

Myth 3: Dispensationalism Is Inherently Tied to Antinomianism

A third charge is that dispensationalism is inherently linked with antinomianism. Antinomianism, as Robert D. Linder defines, is "the doctrine that it is not necessary for Christians to preach and/or obey the moral law of the OT."[41] Antinomianism is often associated with the endorsement of lawless behavior.[42]

According to Gerstner, dispensationalism is "committed to the non-negotiable doctrine of Antinomianism."[43] To him, "all traditional dispensationalists teach that converted Christian persons *can* (not may) live in sin throughout their postconversion lives with no threat to their eternal destiny."[44]

---

[39] C. Norman Kraus, *Dispensationalism in America* (Richmond: John Knox, 1958), 59.

[40] Wayne Grudem, *Systematic Theology: An Introduction to Biblical Doctrine* (Grand Rapids: Zondervan, 1994), 338.

[41] Robert D. Linder, "Antinomianism," *Evangelical Dictionary of Theology*, ed. Walter A. Elwell (Grand Rapids: Baker, 1984), 57. The term comes from the Greek *anti* (against) and *nomos* (law).

[42] See Robert A. Pyne, "Antinomianism and Dispensationalism," *Bibliotheca Sacra* 153 (April-June 1996): 141.

[43] Gerstner, v.

[44] Ibid., 240.

Gerstner went beyond simply arguing that certain dispensationalists teach antinomianism. To him, dispensationalism is inherently antinomian.[45] Gerstner believes dispensationalism is antinomian because of its assertion that the Christian is not under the Mosaic Law and because of its alleged failure "to understand the Reformation doctrines of justification and sanctification."[46] Dispensationalists, he claims, believe that people can be justified without becoming sanctified. This "dualism" according to Gerstner, leads to the belief that Christians can be "carnal."[47]

Gerstner is correct that some dispensationalists have separated justification from sanctification. And this is unfortunate. We must, however, address other issues as well. Are there leading dispensationalists who see justification and sanctification as being inseparable? Also, must dispensationalism drive a dispensationalist to separate justification from sanctification?

Contrary to Gerstner's claim, many dispensationalists see an inseparable connection between justification and sanctification (like myself), and many do not accept that a person can be justified without also being sanctified. Not only is there nothing within dispensationalism that would cause a dispensationalist to separate justification from sanctification, many dispensationalists view justification and sanctification as inseparable. John MacArthur, for example, argues explicitly against antinomianism and for the view that justification and sanctification are inseparable.[48] For MacArthur, "There is no such thing as a true convert to Christ who is justified but who is not being sanctified."[49] This position is not recent to dispensationalism.

---

[45] As R. C. Sproul writes, "One of the most serious charges Gerstner levels at Dispensationalism is the charge that its system of theology is inherently antinomian." Gerstner, *Wrongly Dividing the Word of Truth*, with a foreword by R. C. Sproul, x.

[46] Gerstner, 244.

[47] Ibid., 245.

[48] MacArthur, *Faith Works*, 93–98.

[49] Ibid., 114.

The dispensationalist Donald G. Barnhouse declared, "Justification and sanctification are as inseparable as a torso and a head. You can't have one without the other."[50] Alva J. McClain stated, "Justification cannot be separated from sanctification." He also said, "Justification and sanctification are two aspects of the one work of God in saving men."[51]

Like Gerstner, Curtis Crenshaw and Grover Gunn also assert that there is "an antinomianism inherent in Dispensationalism."[52] To them, dispensationalists reject God's moral law and hold that Christians are free to act carnally:

> Rejecting the moral law, especially OT moral law, results in a number of consequences. They tend to reject the idea that Christ is ruling now by His law (or any law for that matter) as King of kings, relegating this to a future millennium. This in turn leads them to reject His Lordship in salvation and maintain that one can have faith without works (the carnal Christian idea).[53]

There are two other responses to this charge of antinomianism. First, we are not denying that some dispensationalists may have antinomian tendencies (although we know of no dispensationalist who actually advocates lawless living). We deny, though, that dispensationalism itself is inherently antinomian. A system that is primarily concerned with ecclesiology and eschatology cannot necessarily lead to antinomianism. As Feinberg puts it:

> Some argue that Dispensationalism entails antinomianism, since dispensationalists claim that the law is done

---

[50] Donald G. Barnhouse, *Romans*, Vol. 3 (Grand Rapids: Eerdmans, 1961), 10–12.

[51] Alva J. McClain, *Romans: The Gospel of God's Grace* (Winona Lake: BMH, 1973), 141.

[52] Curtis Crenshaw and Grover E. Gunn, *Dispensationalism Today, Yesterday, and Tomorrow* (Memphis: Footstool, 1985; reprint, 1995), 92.

[53] Ibid., 83–84.

away, for Christ is the end of the law (Rom. 10:4). Though some may hold this view, it is hardly the norm or necessitated by Dispensationalism.[54]

MacArthur, too, is correct when he says, "It is a gross misunderstanding to assume that antinomianism is at the heart of dispensationalist doctrine."[55]

Second, although most dispensationalists claim that Christians today are not under the Mosaic Law, they do not assert that Christians are without *any* law. Crenshaw and Gunn's claim that dispensationalists reject "moral law" is a misrepresentation of what dispensationalists believe. Many dispensationalists believe that Christians today are under a new law— the Law of Christ, in which the moral laws of God are communicated. According to Wayne G. Strickland, the Law of Christ "is the new covenant counterpart to the Mosaic Law. Just as the Mosaic Law was normative for the Jew, the law of Christ is binding for the Christian."[56] According to Blaising, dispensationalism is not antinomian because "while it teaches that Mosaic covenant law has ended dispensationally, it also teaches that it has been replaced by new covenant law."[57] In his summary of the dispensational view of the law, Erickson

---

[54] Feinberg, "Systems of Discontinuity," 71.

[55] MacArthur, *Faith Works*, 225. According to MacArthur, "The men who taught me in seminary were all dispensationalists. Yet none of them would have defended no-lordship teaching." 225.

[56] Wayne G. Strickland, "The Inauguration of the Law of Christ With the Gospel of Christ: A Dispensational View," in *The Law, The Gospel, and the Modern Christian: Five Views*, ed. Wayne G. Strickland (Grand Rapids: Zondervan, 1993), 277; Feinberg writes, "Dispensationalists claim that the believer is under the Law of Christ as outlined in the NT. As in the case of the Mosaic Code, the Law of Christ embodies the timelessly true moral principles of God which are instantiated in both codes. But as a separate code the Law of Christ excludes the ceremonial and civil aspects of the Mosaic Code. Dispensationalism is neither antinomian nor entails it." Feinberg, "Systems of Discontinuity," 71.

[57] Blaising and Bock, *Progressive Dispensationalism*, 199. Strickland also states, "The moral law expressed in the Mosaic law under the old covenant has its parallel in the law of Christ under the new covenant, so that the believer today may know God's moral will." "The Inauguration of the Law of Christ With the Gospel of Christ: A Dispensational View," 277.

writes, "The moral law is always in effect . . . although its exact content may vary."[58]

One can argue dispensationalists are in error concerning the Mosaic Law and the Law of Christ, but it is not accurate to charge dispensationalism with teaching Christians today have no law or that Christians can sin with no worry. It should also be noted that the historical connection between dispensationalism and antinomianism is overstated. As an expert in the history of dispensationalism, Blaising writes, "I am not convinced by Gerstner that Antinomianism as traditionally understood is representative of dispensationalism."[59]

Myth 4: Dispensationalism Leads to Non-lordship Salvation

A fourth charge against dispensationalism is that it necessarily leads to a non-lordship view of salvation. Although taking different forms, non-lordship theology is usually characterized by the beliefs that repentance and surrender of one's life to the lordship of Christ are not necessary for salvation to occur. Some non-lordship advocates also hold that a person can be saved and not evidence spiritual fruit.[60]

---

[58] Erickson, *A Basic Guide to Eschatology*, 110.

[59] Craig A. Blaising, "Dispensationalism: The Search for Definition," *Dispensationalism, Israel and the Church*, 14, n.3.

[60] According to Belcher, there are six main characteristics of non-lordship theology: (1) the call to salvation and the call to discipleship are distinct; (2) the believer has the choice to produce or not produce fruit in his life; (3) lack of spiritual fruit is no sign a person is lost; (4) repentance is not a condition of salvation; (5) the concept of lordship is not a condition of salvation but should follow the experience of salvation by faith; and (6) those who possess true saving faith can live in habitual sin or even apostatize from the faith. Richard P. Belcher, *A Layman's Guide to the Lordship Controversy* (Southbridge, MA: Crowne Publications, 1990), 22–23.

According to Gerstner, "All this dispensational defection from the gospel has come to a head in the Lordship controversy."[61] To him, "The gospel of dispensational Antinomianism declares that a person may have Christ as Savior but refuse to accept Him as Lord of one's life."[62]

Clearly, some dispensationalists hold to a non-lordship view of salvation or have non-lordship tendencies. Lewis Sperry Chafer, for example, made statements compatible with a non-lordship view.[63] The most well-known advocate of non-lordship theology is Zane Hodges. His books, *The Gospel Under Siege* and *Absolutely Free* are explicit promotions of non-lordship theology.[64] In my opinion these books have serious errors. But again, the issue here is not whether some dispensationalists have held to a non-lordship view, but whether the non-lordship view is a necessary result of dispensationalism. We assert that it is not for two reasons.

First, since dispensationalism is primarily about ecclesiology and eschatology, it does not have a necessary connection to the lordship issue which is a soteriological matter. Dispensationalists even challenge whether the more extreme non-lordship view of some dispensationalists is even historically related to dispensationalism. Saucy, for example, claims, "The radical non-lordship position of some contemporary dispensationalists, denying the need in salvation of a 'faith that works' based on James 2:14–26, has never been a part of traditional or classical dispensationalism."[65]

Second, several leading dispensational theologians have explicitly rejected the non-lordship view. John MacArthur and Robert Saucy, for example, have openly argued against the

---

[61] Gerstner, 293.

[62] Ibid., 292.

[63] Chafer said, "The error of imposing Christ's Lordship upon the unsaved is disastrous. . . ." Lewis Sperry Chafer, *Systematic Theology*. Vol. 3. (Dallas: Dallas Seminary Press, 1948), 385.

[64] Zane Hodges, *The Gospel Under Siege: Faith and Works in Tension*, 2d ed. (Dallas: Redencion Viva, 1992); *Absolutely Free!* (Dallas: Redencion Viva, 1989).

[65] Saucy, *The Case for Progressive Dispensationalism*, 16, n. 7.

non-lordship position as espoused by Hodges.[66] Interestingly, in his assertion that dispensationalism is inherently connected to the non-lordship view, Gerstner cites John MacArthur against other dispensationalists.[67] But the logic here is odd. Gerstner cites the dispensationalist, John MacArthur, to show that dispensationalism's alleged non-lordship view is wrong. Instead of proving Gerstner's point, though, his use of MacArthur shows that there is diversity within dispensationalism on this issue and that there is no inherent connection between dispensationalism and non-lordship theology.

Myth 5: Dispensationalism Is Primarily about Seven Dispensations

While affirming that salvation is always by grace through faith alone, dispensationalists have often tried to identify the various ways God has worked in history, noting that there are several dispensations in redemptive history. One explicit example is the Mosaic dispensation between Moses and Jesus when the Mosaic Law was operative for the people of Israel. This was followed by the era of the church in Christ, characterized by Holy Spirit indwelling and freedom from the Mosaic Law. The difference between the two eras is seen in John 1:17: "For the Law was given through Moses; grace and truth were realized through Jesus Christ." With Ephesians 1:10 Paul speaks of a future kingdom era when he says, "with a view to an administration [*oikonomia*] suitable to the fullness of the times, that is, the summing up of all things in Christ, things in the heavens and things upon the earth." So there are different and identifiable eras in the unfolding of history. Four are clearly evident although more than four certainly exist—(1) Adam to Moses; (2) Moses to Christ (i.e. Law); (3) Christ's first

---

[66] Saucy refers to the "error of non-lordship salvation.'" Saucy, *The Case for Progressive Dispensationalism*, 15–16, n. 8; See MacArthur's book, *Faith Works.*

[67] Gerstner, 294–95.

coming to His second coming (i.e. the church), and (4) Jesus' kingdom after His second coming.

Through the use of charts dispensationalists have often drawn attention to the differing dispensations in history. This has occurred so much that the thought of "charts" often accompanies the title "dispensationalism" in the minds of many. Clarence Larkin (1850–1924), for example, was famous for offering multiple complex charts that depicted in detail God's purposes in history.

The biblical term, *oikonomia*, means "administration" and "stewardship" involving how a head of household manages the people and matters under his authority. In regard to God, an *oikonomia* can refer to how God is working with His creation in a certain era of history (see Eph. 1:10).

But how essential are dispensations to dispensationalism? Since dispensationalism is often linked with the concept of dispensations and belief in seven dispensations, some have concluded that belief in seven dispensations is essential to the dispensational system. This claim, though, is not accurate. Dispensationalism is not primarily about believing in dispensations or believing in seven dispensations. Why is this the case?

First, believing in dispensations cannot be a distinguishing characteristic of dispensationalism since all Christians believe in dispensations, and Christians before the rise of dispensationalism affirmed various dispensations in God's purposes. What Christian does not believe there is a dispensational difference between the pre-fall and post-fall world? Who does not acknowledge that the present age is different from the coming new heaven and new earth? In addition, dispensationalists were not the first to invent dispensational charts. Several theologians have charted God's various workings in history.

Dispensationalism also is not about acknowledging the Greek term *oikonomia*. After all, what scholar does not believe *oikonomia* is a biblical term? Acknowledging the word *oikonomia* does not make one a dispensationalist, nor does defining this term reveal to us the essence of dispensationalism. As John Feinberg pointed out, "The initial error is thinking that the word 'dispensation' and talk of differing administrative orders only appears in dispensational thinking."[68] Feinberg is also correct that, "Defining the term 'dispensation' no more defines the essence of Dispensationalism than defining the term 'covenant' explains the essence of Covenant Theology."[69]

In a similar way, the number of dispensations is not essential to dispensationalism. Traditionally, dispensationalism has been linked with belief in "seven" dispensations. *The Scofield Reference Bible*, for example, promoted seven dispensations. But others have posited four or eight or some other number. Personally, I disagree with the omission of the Tribulation Period and Eternal State in some dispensational presentations. Plus, I do not affirm a strict "test-failure-judgment" criteria for determining a dispensation, which was often a part of earlier dispensationalism. This seems too narrow and overly focused on man's failures in history without properly taking into account the progress God is making in history. The "test-failure-judgment," model, while having some merit, also omits dispensations that appear obvious like the coming Tribulation Period and the Eternal State.

My understanding is that a dispensation is a noticeable era when God administers and deals with His creation in a unique way. Criteria for a dispensation can involve such matters as the giving of a covenant, a covenant head such as Noah and Abraham, more revelation being offered, or certain blessings and consequences being presented. It could be an era such as the Tribulation Period when God unleashes His wrath upon an unbelieving world in preparation for His kingdom.

Some dispensations may reveal a test-failure-judgment pattern, but this should not be the sole criteria for a dispensation. Since the Bible does not offer specific criteria for understanding a dispensation, we should be flexible in offering and evaluating dispensations. Thus, I do not believe one must hold to seven dispensations to be a true dispensationalist. Feinberg

---

[68] John Feinberg, "Systems of Discontinuity," 69.

[69] Ibid., 69.

is correct again when he states, "The number of dispensations is not at the heart of the system."[70]

The study of dispensations is a worthy endeavor. But I do not believe the issues of how many dispensations there are and what they should be called are at the heart of the dispensational system.

Other Myths

There are other myths about dispensationalism that could be addressed as well, some of which may have been defining points of dispensationalism in its earlier stages. One is the assumption that dispensationalism necessarily teaches that the Sermon on the Mount applies only to the future millennial kingdom. Lewis Sperry Chafer held this view,[71] and it is true that earlier dispensationalists relegated the Sermon on the Mount (Matthew 5–7) to the future millennium. But most dispensationalists today do not hold this view. Most dispensationalists today see the Sermon on the Mount as a kingdom ethic that certainly is applicable to today.[72]

Another myth is that dispensationalism teaches a difference between the kingdom of God and kingdom of heaven. This view was held by some earlier dispensationalists but is largely rejected by more recent dispensationalists. A distinction needs to be made between what certain dispensationalists believe and what is inherent to the system. As John Martin has observed, "One of the greatest misunderstandings is an assumption that there is a single 'dispensational interpretation' of every passage."[73]

Other claims about dispensationalism reach the level of absurd. Popular radio host Hank Hanegraaff claimed in his

---

[70] Ibid., 70.

[71] Lewis S. Chafer, *Systematic Theology* (Dallas: Dallas Seminary Press, 1948), 5:98.

[72] See John A. Martin, "Christ, the Fulfillment of the Law in the Sermon on the Mount," in *Dispensationalism, Israel and the Church*, 248–263.

[73] Ibid., 249, n. 2.

book, *Apocalypse Code*, that dispensationalism's view of a literal fulfillment of land promises to Israel and belief that Israel will undergo tribulation in the future leads to racism and the promotion of ethnic cleansing.[74] This accusation is silly. Dispensationalists believe in a restoration of Israel and a future tribulation period because they believe the Bible teaches these things. This hardly leads to racism. To use an example, Jesus predicted the destruction of Jerusalem in A.D. 70 in Luke 19:41–44 and Luke 21:20–24. If you lived in the 30s A.D. and believed Jesus' words would that make you a racist? Of course not! Also, in the Old Testament God explicitly chose Israel from all the nations (see Deut. 7:6). Was God a racist in the Old Testament since He chose ethnic Israel for service in a way that He did not with other peoples of the earth?

Stephen Sizer, in his book, *Zion's Christian Soldiers*, also makes an outlandish assertion that dispensational beliefs result in a total lack of concern of major national and global issues:

> Sadly, the mistaken idea of a secret rapture has generated a lot of bad theology. It is probably the reason why many Christians don't seem to care about climate change or about preserving diminishing supplies of natural resources. They are similarly not worried about the national debt, nuclear war, or world poverty, because they hope to be raptured to heaven and avoid suffering the consequences of the coming global holocaust.[75]

The real sad issue is that Sizer would make such a statement. Dispensationalists today believe that the Christian worldview should be applied to all areas of our environment, and this includes interest in social and political matters. Many

---

[74] Hank Hanegraaff, *Apocalypse Code: Find Out What the Bible Really Says about the End Times and Why It Matters Today* (Nashville: Thomas Nelson, 2007), xx–xxii.

[75] Stephen Sizer, *Zion's Christian Soldiers?* (Nottingham, England: Inter-Varsity, 2007), 136–37.

Christian organizations and schools that are the most influential on a cultural and political level today have a foundation in dispensational theology. As a dispensationalist I do care about nuclear weapons, national debt, natural resources and the other things Sizer mentions. The same is true for most of the dispensationalists I know. Again, this appears to be a case where a person thinks he understands the implications of dispensationalism but really does not.

In sum, the points stated above are myths about dispensationalism. Those studying dispensationalism should focus on the real issues and avoid such false ideas.

4

Continuity and Discontinuity In Dispensationalism

Theology systems often can be placed on a continuity-discontinuity spectrum or scale. "Continuity," in this context, refers to a connection or carryover of an Old Testament idea or concept into the New Testament. For example the fact that salvation has always been by grace alone through faith alone is evidence of continuity between the Old and New Testaments (Rom. 4:1–8). "Discontinuity" refers to a change or disconnect between the Old Testament and New Testament. For example, New Testament saints do not offer Mosaic Law sacrifices today. Most theologians acknowledge that God's purposes include various elements of continuity and discontinuity. How much of each is heavily debated.

Dispensationalism is often known as a "discontinuity" system, mostly because it sees a distinction between Israel and the church. In the very important and helpful book, *Continuity and Discontinuity*, edited by John S. Feinberg,[1] dispensationalism was identified as a discontinuity system, mostly because it sees a significant distinction between Israel and the church.

---

[1] John S. Feinberg, "Systems of Discontinuity," *Continuity and Discontinuity: Perspectives on the Relationship Between the Old and New Testaments*, ed. John S. Feinberg (Wheaton, IL: Crossway, 1988).

Continuity in Dispensationalism

But while affirming important areas of discontinuity in the testaments, dispensationalism also affirms significant areas of continuity. Below are areas where dispensationalism affirms continuity between the Old Testament and New Testament. Note that each of these eight points below could be developed over many pages, but for the sake of brevity I list them with a short explanation.

1. Storyline Continuity Dispensationalists believe there is strong continuity between the storyline of the Old Testament and the storyline presented in the New Testament. While the New Testament adds details to the Bible's storyline it does not change the story. It does not alter the trajectory of what came before. Dispensationalists believe the covenants, promises, and prophecies of the Old Testament are and will be fulfilled literally through the two comings of Jesus. This includes all physical and spiritual realities along with all particular (Israel, Israel's land) and universal entities (all nations, their lands). While affirming the importance of spiritual realities such as salvation, forgiveness, new heart, and indwelling Holy Spirit, dispensationalists do not believe physical realities are spiritualized or transcended with the coming of Jesus and the New Testament era. This contrasts with non-dispensational systems which often see the New Testament as *transcending, transforming, transposing,* or *spiritualizing* the message of the Old Testament.[2] To repeat, dispensationalism affirms that the storyline begun in the Old Testament is fulfilled literally through the two comings of Jesus. The story does not change. This includes many

---

[2] For example, Beale states, "Thus, the NT storyline will be a *transformation* of the OT one in the light of how the NT is seen to be an unfolding of the OT." G. K. Beale, *A New Testament Biblical Theology: The Unfolding of the Old Testament in the New* (Grand Rapids: Baker Academic, 2011), 6. Stephen Wellum says that with the coming of Jesus, "many of the themes that were basic to the Old Testament have now been *transposed and transformed.*" Peter J. Gentry and Stephen J. Wellum, *Kingdom through Covenant: A Biblical-Theological Understanding of the Covenants* (Wheaton, IL: Crossway, 2012), 598. Emphases in the above quotations are mine.

realities concerning the Messiah and His role, Israel, the land, Jerusalem, the temple, nations, etc.

2. **The Messiah's kingdom is consistent with the kingdom promised in the Old Testament**. The Prophets and Psalms predicted a future earthly kingdom of the Messiah where He transforms the planet and rules the literal nations of the world (Ps. 2; 72; 110; Isa. 2, 11, 25). Dispensationalists see these predictions coming to fulfillment as a result of the second coming of Jesus the Messiah. Just as the Old Testament promised a future tangible earthly kingdom over the nations, so too does the New Testament (Matt. 19:28; Rev. 19:15). The kingdom is not spiritualized or transcended. Thus, when John the Baptist and Jesus declared, "The kingdom of heaven is at hand" (Matt. 3:2; 4:17) they meant the prophesied earthly kingdom foretold in the Old Testament. This is in contrast to some non-dispensational systems that often see the promised earthly kingdom of the Old Testament spiritualized to a present reign of the Messiah from heaven.

3. **Israel**. Israel of the Old Testament consists of the ethnic descendants of Abraham, Isaac, and Jacob that comprise the nation of Israel. Sometimes these Israelites are saved and sometimes they are not. Likewise, all 73 references to "Israel" in the New Testament refer to ethnic Israelites or ethnic Israelites who have believed in Jesus ("Israel of God" Gal. 6:16). There is no transformation or transcending of the concept of Israel. There is no enlargement or expansion of Israel to include Gentiles, although there is expansion of the "people of God" concept to include believing Gentiles alongside believing Israelites (Eph. 2:11–22). Thus, "Israel" in the New Testament carries the meaning of Israel found in the Old Testament. This is in contrast to non-dispensational systems that often view Israel as being redefined, enlarged, or transcended to include Gentiles.

4. **Israel's land and Jerusalem**. Israel's land and Jerusalem continue to remain significant in New Testament times. Jesus offers instructions for people living in Judea in the last days and anticipates a coming restoration of Jerusalem (Matt 24:15–22; Luke 21:24). Thus, this is another area where dispensationalism affirms continuity.

5. **Day of the Lord**. The coming Day of the Lord that impacts both the land of Israel and the entire world is taught in the New Testament as well as the Old Testament (Isa. 13; 1 Thess. 5; 2 Thess. 2). The Old Testament prophets predicted that the Day of the Lord would involve the judgment of the nations, the regathering of Israel, and an earthly kingdom following judgment (Isa. 24–27). This scenario is affirmed in the New Testament (Matt. 24–25).

6. **Messianic salvation extending to believing Gentiles**. The Old Testament predicted that Gentiles would become the people of God because of the Messiah (Amos 9:11–12) and that has happened in New Testament times (Acts 15:14–18). The coming of Jesus means that Gentiles have been included in the covenants of promise and have a relationship to the Messiah just as believing Israelites do (see Eph. 2:11–3:6).

7. **Salvation by grace alone through faith alone**. Dispensationalism affirms that salvation in all ages is by grace alone through faith alone (Gen. 15:6; Rom. 4). While the content of biblical revelation increases throughout the canon there is great continuity regarding salvation. Old Testament saints and New Testament saints are saved by grace alone, through faith alone, based on the atonement of Jesus. As argued earlier, the claim that dispensationalism teaches multiple ways of salvation is false.

8. The New Testament quotes and alludes to the Old Testament in ways consistent with the original literal meaning of the Old Testament writers. There are approximately 350 quotations of the Old Testament in the New Testament. While there are some challenging cases, the vast majority of Old Testament uses in the New Testament are contextual and consistent with the ideas of the Old Testament writers. This fact emphasizes continuity between the storyline of the Old Testament and that found in the New Testament. Dispensationalists may vary to some degree on New Testament use of the Old Testament but overall most affirm continuity between Old Testament meaning and New Testament usage of the Old Testament.

Summary

These are just some areas of continuity within dispensationalism. Contrary to what some critics claim, dispensationalism does not start with the concept of "discontinuity" and impose it on the Bible to find what it wants to find.

Because I see much continuity in dispensationalism I would not identify this system as solely a discontinuity system. I believe dispensationalism is a healthy and biblical balance of both continuity and discontinuity. I will now comment more on the discontinuity elements below.

Discontinuity in Dispensationalism

There are five major areas of discontinuity to note in dispensationalism. Again, the goal here is not to be exhaustive on this topic but to point out major areas of discontinuity within dispensationalism as a point of reference for understanding and evaluating dispensationalism.

1. Israel and the church. Dispensationalism affirms the biblical distinction between Israel and the church. Israel consists of the physical descendants of Abraham, Isaac, and Jacob that comprise the nation Israel. Some Israelites are saved and some are not, but Israel always has an ethnic component in the Bible. The church, on the other hand, is the new covenant community of believing Jews and Gentiles in this age who have believed in Jesus the Messiah. The church includes believing Israelites ("Israel of God" Gal. 6:16; Rom. 9:6) but is not the same thing as "Israel." With the 73 references to "Israel" in the New Testament none refer to the church, nor are Gentiles ever referred to as "Israel." Dispensationalism affirms that Israel is a vehicle for bringing blessings to Gentiles (see Gen. 12:2–3), but it is not God's intent to make Gentiles part of Israel.

From Exodus 19 onward the nation Israel was the mediatorial vehicle for God's purposes in the world. Yet with Israel's failure, culminating in Israel's rejection of her own Messiah, the church became God's vehicle for gospel and kingdom proclamation in this age between the two comings of Jesus. God is still saving a remnant of Israelites (Rom. 11:1–6), but in this age the church is the messenger of God's kingdom program, taking the gospel to all nations. When God saves the mass of national Israel in the future (Rom. 11:26) Israel will once again have a mediatorial role of service and leadership to the nations under Jesus the Messiah who at that time will be ruling the nations (Isa. 2:2–4; Matt. 19:28; Rev. 19:15). But in this age the church is the primary agent for God's kingdom purposes.

Israel has deep roots in the Old Testament. But the church is linked with all who have believed in Jesus the Messiah and have experienced the new covenant ministry of the Holy Spirit. Thus, the church began on the Day of Pentecost when the Holy Spirit came upon the followers of Jesus (Acts 2). Some want to make the "church" the people of God of all ages but that is not correct. Jesus and the new covenant are the main ingredients for the church and only New Testament saints have experienced these yet.

2. Mosaic Covenant to New Covenant. The Mosaic covenant was a temporary and conditional covenant given to Israel at Mount Sinai (Exodus 19). The era of the Mosaic covenant ended with Jesus' death and the establishment of the new covenant (Eph. 2:15; Heb. 8:8–13). Most dispensationalists hold that the Mosaic covenant was a unit that ended with the death of Christ. We are now under Jesus' priesthood associated with the new covenant, not the Aaronic priesthood of the Mosaic covenant. As the writer of Hebrews stated, "when the priesthood is changed, of necessity there takes place a change of law also" (Heb.7:12). As a result dispensationalists believe Christians are under the new covenant, not the Mosaic covenant. Likewise Christians are under the Law of Christ as our code for life, not the Mosaic Law. This Law of Christ has many similarities with the Law of Moses since God's moral standards remain constant, but the Christian is no longer bond by the Mosaic Law as a rule for life. With 1 Corinthians 9:20–21 Paul explicitly stated he was under the Law of Christ, not the Mosaic Law.

3. Dispensations Like all Christians, dispensationalists believe in dispensations—eras in which God works with His people in different ways. The pre-fall era with Adam and Eve was obviously different than the post-fall era. The present church age is different from Israel's previous theocracy under the Mosaic covenant. The kingdom that follows Jesus' return will differ in some ways from the present age we live in as Jesus rules from and over the earth (Zech. 14:9). Yet even with differences among these dispensations, salvation has always been by grace alone, through faith alone, based on the atonement of Jesus. Dispensations may change but the way a person is saved always remains the same (Gen. 15:16; Rom. 4).

Dispensationalists debate the number and characteristics that make up the various dispensations (as non-dispensationalists also do), but they acknowledge that God has worked in different ways at different times. Yet the way of salvation remains the same throughout history. Thus, the dispensations evidence both continuity and discontinuity.

4. People of God The concept of the people of God has varied throughout some dispensations. To be clear—all God's people from beginning to end are saved the same way (i.e. continuity), but the people of God concept has varied. From Adam until Moses there was no nation of Israel so the people of God were not related to any one nation. According to Paul this was also an era in which people were sinners even though they did not have special specific verbal revelation that Adam and Moses had (see Rom. 5:13–14).

With Israel becoming a nation, the people of God concept was strongly linked with Israel and the message of salvation coming from Israel. Under the Mosaic covenant era becoming a believer usually meant becoming a proselyte to Israel. Yet because of Jesus and the new covenant, the people of God concept expanded to include believing Gentiles alongside believing Israelites. This expansion of the people of God concept does not mean believing Gentiles become Jews or Israel as non-dispensationalists believe, but they do become the people of God alongside believing Israelites. This is what Paul discusses in Ephesians 2:11–3:6 and what Isaiah predicted in Isaiah 19:24–25 (see also Acts 15:14–18).

5. Role of Holy Spirit Most dispensationalists believe the Holy Spirit's role of permanently indwelling saints began as a result of Jesus' ascension and pouring out of the Holy Spirit as described in Acts 2. Before His death Jesus told the apostles that the Holy Spirit lives with them, but *will be* in them (John 14:17).

In His person and character the Holy Spirit never changes. Yet during Old Testament times He came upon some select persons for temporary indwelling for service (see Exod. 31:3). But His role of permanent indwelling and empowerment of all Christians for sanctification is closely linked with the death and ascension of Jesus the Messiah. This does not deny that the Holy Spirit saved Old Testament saints, but there is greater enablement for sanctification with the coming of the new covenant (see Rom. 8:1–4). Thus, the role of the Holy Spirit is different in the New Testament era.

Summary

Dispensationalism see five areas of discontinuity in the Bible. These areas appear to arise naturally from a grammatical-historical approach to the Bible and are not artificially imposed on the biblical text.

Putting Continuity and Discontinuity Together

To summarize, there are eight areas of continuity and five areas of discontinuity according to dispensationalism:

Continuity in Dispensationalism

1. Storyline Continuity (the storyline of the Old Testament is literally fulfilled over the two comings of Jesus)

2. The kingdom of the Messiah is consistent with the kingdom promised in the Old Testament

3. Israel

4. Israel's land and Jerusalem

5. Day of the Lord

6. Messianic salvation extending to believing Gentiles

7. Salvation by grace alone through faith alone

8. The New Testament quotes and alludes to the Old Testament in ways consistent with the original literal meaning of the Old Testament writers.

Discontinuity in Dispensationalism

1. Israel and the church

2. Mosaic Covenant to New Covenant

3. Dispensations

4. People of God

5. Role of Holy Spirit.

5

Key Differences Between Dispensationalism and Covenant Theology

For the past two centuries dispensationalism and covenant theology have operated as theological rivals within evangelicalism. Covenant theology is a late sixteenth-century development that emphasized various theological covenants as the way to understand God's purposes. Eventually covenant theology became associated with three covenants: (1) covenant of redemption; (2) covenant of works; and (3) covenant of grace. It is not my intent to go into a detailed explanation of covenant theology here, but since covenant theology is the main rival of dispensationalism within evangelicalism, I want to explain what I think are the key differences between the two systems.

Both dispensationalism and covenant theology have rich traditions and excellent theologians and defenders. Much has been written about these two theological systems. But what are the real issues that separate dispensationalism and covenant theology?

The issues involving these systems are many and complex and I cannot cover a lot of important areas, but below is a thumbnail summary of what I think are the most fundamental differences between these two systems of theology.

85

What the Issues Are Not

But first I offer some comments on what are *not* key differences. Significantly, the gospel is not a dividing issue between dispensationalism and covenant theology. Both sides affirm that salvation can only be found in Jesus Christ alone through faith alone. This agreement on the gospel should be celebrated. Whatever differences exist between these systems the gospel is not one of them. Dispensationalists and covenant theologians are brothers in Christ.

Next, the issue of dispensations, in my opinion, is not a fundamental point of difference. This might surprise some since dispensationalism is closely connected to the idea of dispensations. But covenantalists and dispensationalists both affirm that God has worked in different times and in different ways throughout history (although salvation has always been by grace through faith). Dispensationalists have often spent more energy on the issue of dispensations but this is not the most important factor in my estimation. The two camps may differ on the criteria of a dispensation or how many there are, but belief in dispensations is not the most crucial issue.

Also, the covenants of covenant theology are not what's most important. As mentioned, three covenants have been affirmed in covenant theology—(1) covenant of redemption; (2) covenant of works; and (3) covenant of grace. Yet covenantalists themselves have not agreed on these covenants, some rejecting one or two of these. Plus, they have not always agreed on what these covenants should be called. Also, some dispensationalists have affirmed one or all three of these covenants while remaining dispensationalists. So I don't believe the covenants of covenant theology are the main issues separating the two systems.

So if the dispensations of dispensationalism and the covenants of covenant theology are not at the heart of the differences between the two camps, what are the main differences? The answer comes down to two matters—*hermeneutics* and *storyline*.

Hermeneutics

Hermeneutics deals with principles for Bible interpretation. Dispensationalists affirm a consistent historical-grammatical or literal hermeneutic applied to all areas of Scripture, including eschatology (end times) and Old Testament passages related to national Israel. This approach includes a literal understanding of passages concerning Israel's land, the temple, Jerusalem, etc. Dispensationalism affirms that all details of the Old Testament prophecies, promises, and covenants must be fulfilled in the way the original inspired Bible authors intended. There are no non-literal or spiritual fulfillments of physical and national promises in the Bible. Nor does the New Testament reinterpret, transcend, transform, or spiritualize promises and prophecies in the Old Testament. With dispensationalism, what you see is what you get in the Bible. Its meaning is on the surface. There is no underlying typological trajectory or canonical progression that erases or transcends the Bible's storyline or the significance of the details of the covenants and promises in the Bible. Historical-grammatical hermeneutics will discover types in the Bible, but the concept of "typological interpretation" that overrides the plain meaning of Bible texts is not accepted in dispensationalism.

While areas like the Mosaic Law are shadows of greater new covenant realities (see Heb. 10:1), dispensationalists do not believe that everything in the Old Testament is a shadow. Matters associated with the covenants of promise including Israel, Israel's land, the temple, Jerusalem, nations, restoration of creation, etc., are not shadows. Promises concerning these matters must be fulfilled as predicted (Matt. 15:18). All of this occurs because of Jesus the Messiah who brings all God's promises to fulfillment (2 Cor. 1:20; Eph. 1:10).

Dispensationalists hold to "passage priority" in which the primary meaning of a passage is found in the passage at hand and not in other passages. Dispensationalists do not believe in the priority of one testament over the other (although the New is more complete), they just ask that the integrity of each passage in each testament be honored without overriding its meaning with other passages. The New Testament will offer newer revelation but it will not contradict or override the meaning of previous passages in the Old Testament. Dispensationalists, therefore, believe all Scripture harmonizes with other Scripture, but no Bible passage transforms, transcends, spiritualizes, redefines, or reinterprets any other Scripture passage.

Covenantalists also affirm a historical-grammatical hermeneutic to many areas of Scripture, but they believe that *typological* and even *spiritual* hermeneutics need to be applied to some areas of scripture—particularly passages involving physical and national promises to national Israel in the Old Testament. These are often viewed as shadows that are transcended by greater New Testament realities (i.e. Jesus and the church).

The covenantal hermeneutic is closely linked to the concept of "New Testament priority" in which the New Testament is viewed as the lens for interpreting and even reinterpreting the Old Testament. This fits with the idea that the transition from the Old Testament to the New Testament is that of shadow to reality. Thus, physical and national promises in the Old Testament are shadows and types that are fulfilled in Jesus and the church. This approach can involve spiritualizing the Old Testament. As Kim Riddlebarger stated, "If the New Testament writers *spiritualize* Old Testament prophecies by *applying them in a nonliteral sense*, then the Old Testament passage must be seen in light of that New Testament interpretation, not vice versa."[1] Allegedly, once the concepts of "Israel" and "temple" find fulfillment in Jesus, one need not expect a literal fulfillment of these matters in the future.

In a nutshell, many of the differences between the two camps concern how literal we should be with physical and na-

---

[1] Kim Riddlebarger, *A Case for Amillennialism: Understanding the End Times* (Grand Rapids: Baker, 2003), 37.

tional promises and covenants in the Old Testament. Dispensationalists view these as realities that need to be fulfilled if they have not been already. Covenantalists often view these as shadows and types that are fulfilled in Jesus with no literal fulfillment of these matters being necessary.

Storyline

In addition to hermeneutics, the other major difference between dispensationalism and covenant theology concerns the Bible's storyline. This involves issues such as the nature of Old Testament promises and covenants, the identity and role of Israel in God's purposes, the identity and role of the church, and what was fulfilled with Jesus' first coming and what remains to be fulfilled with Jesus' second coming.

But when it comes down to it I think the two major storyline differences between the systems concern: (1) the nation Israel's role in God's purposes, and (2) whether there will be a mediatorial kingdom phase to God's kingdom program on earth after this present age but before the Eternal State.

When it comes to Israel, covenantalism perceives Jesus as the true Israel and that Old Testament promises to national Israel in the Old Testament are shadows that find fulfillment in Him. And when all believers, including Gentiles, become united with Christ, they join "Israel" as well. This means the concept of "Israel" expands to include Gentiles. Thus, the church in Jesus is the new/true Israel and the culmination of God's plans for His people. There is no need for a restoration of national Israel since Jesus is "true Israel" and the church in Jesus is now Israel. Also, while acknowledging a "not yet" aspect to Jesus' reign, covenantalists tend to heavily emphasize first coming fulfillment of Old Testament promises and covenants. For most covenantalists Jesus' Davidic/Millennial reign and the reign of the saints is occurring from heaven now. So we are currently in Jesus' messianic kingdom. Also, covenant promises from the Old Testament are mostly being fulfilled now. Thus, there is no need of a future earthly reign of Jesus since this age is the era of fulfillment and reigning.

Dispensationalism, on the other hand, celebrates Jesus' identity and role as the true Israelite, but this truth does not mean the non-significance of the nation Israel. God's plans for Israel involve a role of service for the nation through the "true Israelite"—Jesus the Messiah. Jesus' identity as the true Israelite means the restoration of the nation Israel as Isaiah 49:3–6 teaches. It has always been God's plan for the nation Israel to fulfill a mission of service and leadership to the nations (Gen. 12:2–3; Deut. 4:5–6). Israel failed this mission in the Old Testament, but under Jesus the Messiah, Israel will fulfill its destiny of leadership and service to the nations in a coming messianic kingdom (Isa. 2:2–4). Since nations exist in the coming messianic/millennial kingdom (Isa. 19:24–25; Rev. 19:15), there should be no surprise that Israel as a nation would have a role to the nations during this period—under Jesus the Messiah. Since national Israel is still significant, the church is not a new Israel that supersedes or replaces national Israel in God's purposes. The church is the instrument for gospel and kingdom proclamation in this age, but Israel will still have a role to the nations when Jesus returns to reign over the nations (see Rev. 19:15). The church of this age will also participate in Jesus' rule over the nations (Rev. 2:26-27; 3:21).

Unlike covenantalists, dispensationalists do not believe the concept of "Israel" expands to include Gentiles. Instead, the concept of the "people of God" expands to include believing Gentiles alongside believing Israelites. It is not God's plan for all believers to become Israel, but for there to be ethnic diversity in the people of God as the people of God idea includes both Israelites and Gentiles without either losing their ethnic identities. Even in the Eternal State the people of God are referred to as "the nations" (Rev. 21:24, 26).

Also important to the Bible's storyline, according to dispensationalism, is the necessity of a coming earthly kingdom in which the Last Adam and Messiah will rule the earth successfully for the glory of God. A successful kingdom rule over the earth must occur. God tasked Adam and mankind to rule the earth successfully on His behalf in Genesis 1:26–28, but this kingdom mandate remains unfulfilled as of now, something the writer of Hebrews affirms in Hebrews 2:5–8. Thus, there must be a coming earthly kingdom of Jesus because there must be a successful reign of the Last Adam (Jesus) in the realm where the first Adam failed. Since this reign involves nations, the Messiah will use Israel as an instrument for His kingdom rule during this time. *Thus a coming earthly kingdom reign of Jesus over the nations with Israel as an instrument of His rule is essential to the dispensational understanding of the Bible's storyline.*

Conclusion

Much more could be said on other important differences between dispensationalism and covenant theology but the points mentioned above are at the heart of the differences. Dispensationalists and covenantalists disagree on hermeneutics and the Bible's storyline particularly relating to Israel's role in God's purposes and the necessity of a coming earthly kingdom of the Messiah.

6

Questions and Answers About Dispensationalism

Below are some questions that have been asked about dispensationalism. I answer these in a Question and Answer format.

Question: What is a good short definition of dispensationalism?

Answer: Dispensationalism is a system of theology primarily concerned with the doctrines of ecclesiology and eschatology that emphasizes applying historical-grammatical hermeneutics to all passages of Scripture (including the entire Old Testament). It affirms a distinction between Israel and the church, and a future salvation and restoration of the nation Israel in a future earthly kingdom under Jesus the Messiah as the basis for a worldwide kingdom that brings blessings to all nations.

Question: What is one major contribution dispensationalism makes that separates it from other systems?

Answer: One important contribution of dispensationalism is its understanding that the Bible's storyline, as unfolded in the Old Testament, will be fulfilled literally over the course of Jesus' two comings. Dispensationalism does not spiritualize any of the unconditional and eternal promises and covenants of the

Old Testament. What God led the Bible authors to understand and write will come to literal fulfillment, including what is revealed concerning national Israel. Some Old Testament promises were fulfilled with Jesus' first coming and others await His second coming. But all will be fulfilled just as God promised. Promises that have not been fulfilled yet do not need to be spiritualized or swept under the rug of "typological fulfillment." They will be fulfilled in connection with Jesus' return. *Thus, dispensationalism makes a contribution by rightly understanding that the Bible's storyline as revealed in the Old Testament is the same storyline that is fulfilled in the New Testament over the course of Jesus' two comings. The New Testament does not reinterpret or transcend the Bible's storyline.*

Question: Why are you a dispensationalist and how did you become a dispensationalist?

Answer: I consider myself a dispensationalist because I believe the foundational affirmations of dispensationalism. I accept the hermeneutics of dispensationalism, especially the view that what God promised Israel will be fulfilled with the nation Israel. I also believe its views on the distinction between the church and Israel. My theological heritage as a Christian was influenced by dispensationalism. When I became a Christian at age 14 in the early 1980s I attended dispensational churches. In the early 1990s, though, I examined further the beliefs of my theological heritage to see if dispensationalism lined up with what the Bible teaches. I was aware of the negative critiques that influential non-dispensational scholars had offered. Several reformed and covenantal scholars I had great respect for in the areas of God's sovereignty, salvation, and authority of Scripture were critical of dispensationalism and part of me wondered, "What if they are right? Am I missing something?" I began to examine whether dispensationalism was a biblical theology. I read many books and articles from both sides of the issue. Particularly influential to me was the 1988 book, *Continuity and Discontinuity: Perspectives on the Relationship Between the*

Testaments, edited by John S. Feinberg. The purpose of this book was to put leading dispensational and discontinuity scholars against leading covenant theologians on the important issues of hermeneutics, law, kingdom, people of God, and salvation in the testaments. This book allowed a side-by-side comparison of leading scholars on both sides. And, in my opinion, the dispensational scholars were much more convincing. I found the dispensational hermeneutic of maintaining a reference point in the Old Testament prophetic passages to be correct. I also found the case for a salvation and restoration of the nation Israel to be very strong. The more I studied these issues, the more convinced I became that dispensationalists were right on these important issues. Later, when I wrote my dissertation regarding the relationship between Israel and the church in 2004, I became further convinced that the church is not identified as "Israel" in the Bible and that a future salvation and restoration for Israel was strongly supported in both the Old and New Testaments. Now I am not just a dispensationalist by heritage. I am a convinced dispensationalist from much personal study.

Question: What is the main mistake non-dispensationalists make when evaluating dispensationalism?

Answer: The main mistake is not understanding what dispensationalism is saying and presenting straw man arguments against it. Put simply, many non-dispensational critics are deficient in their understanding of dispensational theology. Whether they are simply overconfident or have not done their homework, they present dispensationalism in a way that is not true or is seriously outmoded. John Gerstner and his book, *Wrongly Dividing the Word of Truth*, was an example of poor research and misrepresentations. By tying dispensationalism to multiple ways of salvation, Arminianism, antinomianism, and non-lordship salvation, Gerstner showed a complete lack of understanding of dispensationalism. Plus, he misrepresented dispensational theology. A recognized principle of scholarship is that one should represent his opponent accurately, and this clearly was not the case with this book. No dispensationalist I knew believed Gerstner was even close to being fair to dispensationalism. Hank Hanegraaff, with his 2007 book, *Apocalypse Code*, was another example of someone pretending to understand dispensationalism, but he too fell far short by making silly claims that dispensationalism threatened the uniqueness of Christ's resurrection and the deity of Christ. Hanegraaff also claimed that dispensationalism leads to racism and the promotion of ethnic cleansing because it believes God will fulfill land promises with the nation Israel and that Israel will undergo tribulation in the future. Fortunately, not many have followed Hanegraaff in making such outrageous claims. Scholars like Anthony Hoekema, Vern Poythress, O. Palmer Robertson, and Willem VanGemeren have been notable exceptions. They deal with real issues and do so in a gracious manner without straw man arguments and personal attacks.

Question: Any other common mistake?

Answer: Yes. Most books critical of dispensationalism often emphasize the dispensationalism of the early twentieth century and do not adequately deal with more recent dispensational scholars. Many say something like, "Dispensationalism is a system of theology that is based on the belief of seven dispensations as found in the *Scofield Reference Bible*." Then a series of documentation comes from scholars from the early twentieth century. I once read a critic of dispensationalism who, while writing in the mid-1990s, refused to deal with the writings of progressive dispensationalists. Why? He said he didn't consider progressive dispensationalists as real dispensationalists. But in doing so he undercut his own credibility. Certainly, quoting earlier dispensational scholars is fair game, but it is also helpful to deal with more recent scholarship as well. A good principle of scholarship is to be aware of both older and recent research on a topic. Yet when reading some critiques of dispensationalism, one gets the impression that dispensational thought was frozen by 1950.

Question: Do you think dispensationalists could do a better job of explaining dispensationalism? If so, how?

Answer: Yes I do. For starters I think dispensationalists have been less than helpful when they emphasize belief in seven dispensations as the starting point for understanding dispensationalism. I don't think that is the real issue and its complicated nature can confuse people. I think the essentials of dispensationalism mentioned in chapter 2 above are better places to start. Second, dispensationalists need to be bolder in defending dispensational beliefs. The Israel/church distinction, premillennialism, and the doctrine of the future salvation and restoration of Israel are very well supported in Scripture. On those issues that are at the heart of dispensationalism, the dispensationalist has much to stand upon. Also, dispensationalism has the most accurate storyline of the various evangelical systems in my opinion. It details God's kingdom purposes for His glory from Genesis 1 through Revelation 22. This should be emphasized more. Thus dispensationalists should focus both on explaining particular passages and explaining God's big-picture purposes.

Question: Many like to point out that dispensationalism began with John Nelson Darby around 1830, thus dispensationalism is a new theology. How do you respond to the charge that dispensationalism should be rejected since it is a new theology?

Answer: I have three responses. First, as mentioned earlier in this book, most of Darby's views were held by other English theologians of the seventeenth and eighteenth centuries. So Darby is not as novel as some claim. Second, it is true that as a system of theology, dispensationalism began in the nineteenth century. Yet it is also true that several key elements of dispensational belief were held by the early church. A strong consensus existed in the Patristic Era (A.D. 100–451) that comings of Elijah and Antichrist would precede the second coming of Jesus. In association with these events there would be a mass conversion of the Jewish people in line with what the Old Testament prophets like Zechariah predicted. Thus, many of the church fathers believed in a future salvation of Israel, something dispensationalists also do. The early church was also clearly premillennial. It believed that Jesus would return a second time to set up an earthly kingdom. The early church also had some views that did not line up with dispensationalism. They often asserted that the church was the new Israel, but this belief did not extinguish their belief in a future salvation for Israel. Because of the early church's views on futurism, premillennialism, and a future salvation for Israel, I believe that the early church was close to dispensationalism. Third, the recent development of dispensationalism must be understood in regard to the development of doctrine in church history. It is often recognized that eschatology was one of the last major doctrines to receive serious and focused attention by the Christian church. The early church focused primarily on the canon of Scripture and the person of Christ. The Reformation Period focused on justification, the sacraments, and what constituted the true church. Yet it would be even later before eschatology received detailed treatment. Covenant theology, the main theological rival to dispensationalism, did not become a mature system until the seventeenth century. If one wants to reject dispensationalism simply for being new, one should also reject covenant theology since it is not much older than dispensationalism. For those looking at the newness of dispensationalism, keep in mind that there were no evangelical eschatological systems until after the Reformation. What we should do is focus on whether any system of theology is biblical or not and not so much on when it started.

Question: What is the relationship between the pre-tribulational rapture position and dispensationalism?

Answer: The pre-tribulational rapture view has traditionally been an important part of dispensationalism. It may even be the most recognizable facet of dispensational theology, and it is a doctrine I believe. It affirms the important biblical truth that the church will be rescued from the Day of the Lord wrath that characterizes the coming seven-year Tribulation period (1 Thess. 4:14–18; Rev. 3:10). The pre-tribulational rapture view is important to dispensationalism, but I do not think the entire system stands or falls on it. Nor would I say it is an essential doctrine of dispensationalism. If I were to receive a note from heaven telling me the pre-tribulational view is not correct, I would still be a dispensationalist because of my views on accepting the integrity of the Old Testament prophetic passages, premillennialism, and the future salvation and restoration of the nation Israel. Interestingly, in their lists of what is at the heart dispensationalism, Charles Ryrie, John Feinberg, and Craig Blaising and Darrell Bock did not list the pre-tribulational rapture view as an essential element of dispensationalism. This is not to downplay the significance of the pre-tribulational rapture view, but it does show that the entire system of dispensationalism does not rest on this one doctrine. To summarize, I personally believe in a pre-tribulational rapture. I think it is an important doctrine, but I would not say dispensationalism is based on this one doctrine.

Question: What is your perspective on the internal debates and discussions within dispensationalism?

Answer: One thing that I like about dispensationalism is that historically its adherents have been willing to make needed modifications. Dispensationalists are willing to examine previous beliefs of earlier dispensationalists to see if these beliefs are biblical or not. Needed changes have been made and there is no circling of the wagons to defend earlier theologians no matter what. For example, some earlier dispensationalists sometimes argued that the church was not related to the new covenant or that there were two new covenants. Later dispensationalists rightly modified these views emphasizing that the church does participate in the new covenant. Some earlier dispensationalists believed that the church and Israel would be separated for eternity, but later dispensationalists rightly revised this view. Today, there are heated debates among dispensationalists over progressive dispensationalism. Some see the progressives as making needed modifications, while others believe they are going too far and have left dispensationalism. My purpose in this book has not been to address the internal debates within dispensationalism. That is a topic for another book. Personally, I think progressive dispensationalists have made some needed modifications and have done an excellent job of refuting replacement theology and noting that there are real fulfillments of some aspects of the covenants of promise today. Yet on other issues they have not been as convincing. The claim Jesus has assumed the Davidic throne in heaven and is reigning from this throne has not been convincing in my opinion. Jesus, on two occasions, stated that He will assume His Davidic throne at the time of His second coming (see Matt. 19:28; 25:31). Like all theological perspectives, we should accept what is biblical and reject what is not. As a dispensationalist, I have learned much from fellow dispensationalists of all kinds, yet I do not have any one dispensational theologian or camp that I would agree with on every single point. Being discerning is important.

Question: Does dispensationalism acknowledge Jesus as "true Israel"?

Answer: Yes, many dispensationalists gladly acknowledge that Jesus is the true and ultimate Israelite. In fact, I have written a journal article affirming that Jesus is the true and ultimate Israelite. It is called, "What Does Christ as 'True Israel' Mean for the Nation Israel?"[1] Based on passages like Isaiah 49, dispensationalists believe Jesus is the true and ultimate Israelite who restores national Israel and brings blessings to the Gentiles. Surprisingly, one critic of dispensationalism said that when it comes to Jesus' identity as true Israel that "Such terminology is frequently attacked in dispensational circles," and then uses me as an example of one who attacks, argues, and complains about this idea.[2] But this is not true. I gladly embrace Jesus as true Israel and know other dispensationalists who do so as well. If there are any who do not like this idea I am not aware of them. The issue between dispensationalists and non-dispensationalists is not whether Jesus is true Israel or not, but what are the implications of Jesus being "true Israel." For non-dispensationalists, Jesus as true Israel means the non-significance of national Israel in God's purposes. For dispensationalists, Jesus' identity as "true Israel" means corporate representation in which the Head (Jesus) restores the many (national Israel). It also means blessings for the Gentiles. Thus, Jesus as the ultimate Israelite means Israel will be restored to complete the mission God intended for the nation (Isa. 2:2–4).

---

[1] Michael J. Vlach, "What Does Christ as 'True Israel' Mean for the Nation Israel?: A Critique of the Non-Dispensational Understanding," *The Master's Seminary Journal* 23/1 (Spring 2012): 43–54.

[2] Brent E. Parker stated: "Such terminology is frequently attacked in dispensational circles. Vlach argues that the language of 'true Israel' is a 'combination of terms [that] is not found in the Bible. Jesus does not call himself "true Israel" and neither do the other NT writers.'" *Progressive Covenantalism: Charting a Course between Dispensational and Covenantal Theologies* (Nashville, TN: B&H Academic), 2016, Kindle Edition, Locations 8484–8486. Parker seems to conclude that since I state accurately that Jesus is not called "true Israel" in those exact words in the Bible that I must fight against this idea. To the contrary I believe the concept of Jesus as "true Israel" exists even though those exact words are not found. Parker also says, "He [Vlach] further complains that calling Jesus 'true Israel' gives the impression that the nation of Israel is not truly Israel anymore" (Kindle Locations 1062–1067). I want to make clear that I do not "complain" about Jesus being true Israel. In this context I asked that Jesus' identity as "true Israel" not be taken to mean national Israel is no longer Israel. I believe in corporate representation in which Jesus as the true Israelite restores the nation Israel. Both are Israel.

Question: What is the future of dispensationalism?

Answer: Dispensationalism has come under heavy criticism in recent years, and being a dispensationalist is not popular these days. Plus, it is becoming increasingly difficult for dispensationalists to publish their works with traditional publishers. In the academic realms of evangelicalism there is a scorn for dispensationalism that I have not seen before. Yet this scorn for dispensationalism has not been earned by defeating dispensationalism with better ideas. There is no book out there that offers a credible refutation of dispensationalism. Instead, victory has been declared without much proof. But in spite of this, I think dispensationalism is alive and well and will remain so. It is interesting to read books and statements from people speaking about the 'breakup,' 'dissolution,' or 'death' of dispensationalism. That is simply wishful thinking from those strongly opposed to dispensationalism and more of a case of what they wish were true instead of what is really true. There are still many colleges, seminaries, and Bible teachers that affirm the essentials of dispensationalism. In the seminary classes I teach I see excitement when students learn what God's Word says about the future including the millennium and God's plans for both Israel and the church. I expect that ongoing debates between traditional and progressive dispensationalists will continue, and this is a good thing. Every belief should be examined and reexamined to make sure it is biblical. Yet, the basic beliefs of dispensational theology find their basis in the Bible and these truths will continue to be held by many in the church. Those who hold to dispensational ideas need to value truth more than being popular in the academic realm.

Conclusion

This book has surveyed essential beliefs and common myths associated with dispensationalism. As a system of theology dispensationalism offers significant claims that are worthy of evaluation. Unfortunately, discussions concerning dispensationalism are often accompanied by two errors. The first is linking dispensationalism with issues not really related to dispensationalism. The most obvious violation here is connecting dispensationalism with multiple ways of salvation, Arminianism, antinomianism, and non-lordship salvation. But as discussed, dispensationalism is primarily about ecclesiology, eschatology, and testament priority.

The second error involves treating secondary beliefs of dispensationalism as foundational and evaluating the validity of dispensationalism on these beliefs. Feinberg is correct that "both proponents and critics [of dispensationalism] have too often treated applications of the system like foundational principles."[1] For example, showing that the Sermon on the Mount is for today or showing that the kingdom of God and kingdom of heaven are the same does not defeat dispensationalism. The same is true for belief in seven dispensations.

To summarize, dispensationalism is rooted in six basic beliefs that are at the heart of the system:

1. The primary meaning of any Bible passage is found in that passage. The New Testament does not reinterpret or transcend Old Testament passages in a way that overrides or

---

[1] John S. Feinberg, "Systems of Discontinuity," *Continuity and Discontinuity: Perspectives on the Relationship Between the Old and New Testaments*, ed. John S. Feinberg (Wheaton, IL: Crossway, 1988), 68.

cancels the original authorial intent of the Old Testament writers.

2. Types exist but national Israel is not an inferior type that is superseded by the church.

3. Israel and the church are distinct, thus the church cannot rightly be identified as the new/true Israel.

4. Spiritual unity in salvation between Jews and Gentiles is compatible with a future functional role for Israel as a nation.

5. The nation Israel will be both saved and restored with a unique functional role in a future millennial kingdom upon the earth.

6. There are multiple senses of "seed of Abraham," thus the church's identification as "seed of Abraham" does not cancel God's promises to the believing Jewish "seed of Abraham."

For those examining dispensationalism these are the issues that should be emphasized. Proponents of dispensationalism who are involved in discussions with non-dispensationalists should encourage discussion on these issues. Likewise, when non-dispensationalists begin to emphasize other matters like multiple ways of salvation, Arminianism, antinomianism, etc., the dispensationalist should kindly but firmly point out that these are not really at the heart of the issue, and discussion should be redirected to the main issues. Staying focused on the main issues hopefully will elevate the quality of the discussion and the cause of truth will be served well.

Recommended Resources
On Dispensationalism

Sometimes I am asked about which books and articles have most influenced my understanding of dispensationalism. My first answer is the Bible, but below I also note other works that have helped me the most concerning issues such as hermeneutics, law, kingdom, people of God, and other issues. I list around forty such works (including three of my own) that have really helped my understanding of God's Word on important theological issues. There are many more books, articles, chapters, and commentaries that have helped me but I consider these forty below to be the best of the best. For the most part, these resources are positive presentations of biblical issues. I have purposely not included commentaries or works that are refutations of certain views such as amillennialism, postmillennialism, preterism, replacement theology, etc. That is a project for another day. Instead, these works are positive presentations of biblical issues from a dispensational perspective. I do this because the strength of dispensationalism is found in its positive presentation and explanation of biblical issues and that is what I want to focus on here.

I hope the following three categories of readers will learn the following from this list:

Dispensationalists: If you are dispensationalist I hope you will be encouraged from the following works that offer a scholarly but readable presentation of key beliefs associated with dispensational theology. I think your beliefs will be reaffirmed and you will appreciate even more that dispensationalism offers a credible and biblical approach to understanding God's purposes concerning the church, Israel, and the end times.

Opponents of Dispensationalism: If you believe dispensationalism is wrong or dangerous, I ask that you seriously consider these works in your discussions regarding dispensationalism. While we dispensationalists often embrace some or much of what earlier dispensationalists wrote, much has been written in the last thirty years from a dispensational perspective that should also be taken into consideration. It is fair game to talk about Darby, Scofield, Chafer, etc..., but if you do not also engage with Saucy, Feinberg, Turner, Blaising, and Bock and others you are not being fair in your presentations.

The undecided and those in the middle: I hope you consider reading several of these works listed below to get a fair understanding of what dispensationalists believe. Keep in mind that most critics of dispensationalism are not interacting seriously with these works, but that does not mean you have to follow the same path. We are not claiming to be perfect, but I think you will find an honest attempt to be biblical and present an accurate storyline of the Bible

Big Picture Presentations of Dispensationalism

The Case for Progressive Dispensationalism: The Interface Between Dispensational & Non-Dispensational Theology by Robert L. Saucy (Grand Rapids: Zondervan, 1993). (NOTE: A very helpful best book on ecclesiology/eschatology and the covenants. Saucy interacts often with non-dispensationalists on key issues. If I could only recommend one book on ecclesiology/eschatology this would be it.)

Christ's Prophetic Plans: A Futuristic Premillennial Primer (Chicago: Moody, 2012). (NOTE: A clear presentation of dispensational theology from the faculty of The Master's Seminary)

"Systems of Discontinuity," by John S. Feinberg in *Continuity and Discontinuity: Perspectives on the Relationship Between the Old and New Testaments*, ed. John S. Feinberg (Wheaton, IL: Crossway, 1988), 63–86. (NOTE: The best article explaining the essence of dispensationalism in print.)

"Premillennialism," by Craig A. Blaising in *Three Views on the Millennium and Beyond*, ed. Darrell L. Bock (Grand Rapids: Zondervan, 1999), 157–227. (NOTE: A capable defense of premillennialism and how premillennialism is most consistent with a New Creation Model perspective of the kingdom.)

Progressive Dispensationalism by Craig A. Blaising and Darrell L. Bock (Grand Rapids: Baker, 1993). (NOTE: There is much helpful historical and theological information about dispensationalism in this book.)

Hermeneutics of Dispensationalism

"Hermeneutics of Discontinuity," by Paul D. Feinberg in *Continuity and Discontinuity: Perspectives on the Relationship Between the Old and New Testaments*, ed. John S. Feinberg (Wheaton, IL: Crossway, 1988), 109–128. (NOTE: A very capable explanation of dispensational hermeneutics. Paul Feinberg addresses difficult passages such as Acts 2/Joel 2 and Acts 15/Amos 9.)

"Biblical Meaning of 'Fulfillment,'" by Charles H. Dyer in *Issues in Dispensationalism*, eds. Wesley R. Willis and John R. Master (Chicago: Moody, 1994), 51–74. (A very helpful discussion on the meaning of "fulfill" terminology in Matthew.)

"Dispensational Hermeneutics," by Thomas Ice in *Issues in Dispensationalism*, eds. Wesley R. Willis and John R. Master (Chicago: Moody, 1994).

"Israel and Hermeneutics," by Craig A. Blaising in *The People, The Land, and The Future of Israel: Israel and the Jewish People in the Plan of God*, eds. Darrell L. Bock and Mitch Glaser (Grand Rapids: Kregel, 2014), 151–65.

Intertestamental Theological Issues (Law, Kingdom, People of God, etc.)

He Will Reign Forever: A Biblical Theology of the Kingdom of God by Michael J. Vlach (Silverton, OR: Lampion Press, 2017).

"The Law of Moses or The Law of Christ," by Douglas J. Moo in *Continuity and Discontinuity: Perspectives on the Relationship Between the Old and New Testaments*, ed. John S. Feinberg (Wheaton, IL: Crossway, 1988), (NOTE: Moo is not a dispensationalist but he presents a discontinuity view of the Mosaic Law/Law of Christ issue that many dispensationalists share and does so in a compelling way.)

"The Biblical Method of Salvation: A Case for Discontinuity," by Allen P. Ross in *Continuity and Discontinuity: Perspectives on the Relationship Between the Old and New Testaments*, ed. John S. Feinberg (Wheaton, IL: Crossway, 1988), 161–180.

"Israel and the Church: A Case for Discontinuity," by Robert L. Saucy in *Continuity and Discontinuity: Perspectives on the Relationship Between the Old and New Testaments*, ed. John S. Feinberg (Wheaton, IL: Crossway, 1988), 239–262.

The Greatness of the Kingdom: An Inductive Study of the Kingdom of God by Alva J. McClain (Winona Lake, IN: BMH Books, 1959). (NOTE: Simply the best work on the Kingdom. McClain avoids simplistic definitions of the Kingdom and works the reader through the Kingdom program from Genesis 1 through Revelation 22.)

"The Kingdom and Matthew's Gospel," by Stanley D. Toussaint in *Essays in Honor of J. Dwight Pentecost*, eds. Stanley D. Toussaint and Charles H. Dyer (Chicago: Moody, 1986), 19–34.

"The New Covenant and the People(s) of God," by Bruce A. Ware in *Dispensationalism, Israel and the Church: The Search for Definition*, eds. Craig A. Blaising and Darrell Bock (Grand Rapids: Zondervan, 1992), 68–97. (NOTE: A great explanation of how the new covenant applies to the church now but will be fulfilled with Israel in the future.)

"The New Man of Ephesians 2," by Carl B. Hoch, Jr. in *Dispensationalism, Israel and the Church: The Search for Definition*, eds. Craig A. Blaising and Darrell Bock (Grand Rapids: Zondervan,

1992), 98–126. (NOTE: A significant article that shows how spiritual unity between Jews and Gentiles does not rule out a future for ethnic Israel in the future.)

"The Church as the Mystery of God," by Robert L. Saucy in *Dispensationalism, Israel and the Church: The Search for Definition*, eds. Craig A. Blaising and Darrell Bock (Grand Rapids: Zondervan, 1992), 127–155.

"The New Jerusalem in Revelation 21:1–22:5: Consummation of a Biblical Continuum," by David L. Turner in *Dispensationalism, Israel and the Church: The Search for Definition*, eds. Craig A. Blaising and Darrell Bock (Grand Rapids: Zondervan, 1992), 264–292. (NOTE: An important article that shows there may be more continuity between the Millennium and the Eternal State than many think.)

"Israel and the Church," by Arnold G. Fruchtenbaum in *Issues in Dispensationalism*, eds. Wesley R. Willis and John R. Master (Chicago: Moody, 1994), 113–132. (NOTE: A survey of key texts showing the distinction between Israel and the Church.)

"Paul and 'the Israel of God': An Exegetical and Eschatological Case Study," by S. Lewis Johnson, Jr. in *The Master's Seminary Journal*, 20:1 (Spring 2009): 41–55. (NOTE: Johnson refutes the idea that Galatians 6:16 identifies the Church as "Israel.")

"The Significance of the *Syn-Compounds* for Jew-Gentile Relationships in the Body of Christ," by Carl B. Hoch, Jr. in *Journal of the Evangelical Society* 25:2 (1982): 175–183.

"The Contingency of the Coming of the Kingdom," by Stanley D. Toussaint in *Integrity of Heart, Skillfulness of Hands*, eds. Charles H. Dyer and Roy B. Zuck (Grand Rapids: Baker, 1994), 222–237.

Revelation 20 and the Millennial Debate by Matthew Waymeyer (The Woodlands, TX: Kress Christian Publications, 2004).

Bible Books

"Evidence from Isaiah," by John H. Sailhamer in *The Coming Millennial Kingdom: A Case for Premillennial Interpretation*, eds. Donald K. Campbell & Jeffrey L. Townsend (Grand Rapids: Kregel, 1997), 79–102.

"Evidence from Jeremiah," by Walter C. Kaiser in *The Coming Millennial Kingdom: A Case for Premillennial Interpretation*, eds. Donald K. Campbell & Jeffrey L. Townsend (Grand Rapids: Kregel, 1997), 103–118.

"Evidence from Ezekiel," by Mark F. Rooker in *The Coming Millennial Kingdom: A Case for Premillennial Interpretation*, eds. Donald K. Campbell & Jeffrey L. Townsend (Grand Rapids: Kregel, 1997), 119–134.

"Evidence from Joel and Amos," by Homer Heater, Jr. in *The Coming Millennial Kingdom: A Case for Premillennial Interpretation*, eds. Donald K. Campbell & Jeffrey L. Townsend (Grand Rapids: Kregel, 1997), 147–164.

"Evidence from Matthew," by David K. Lowery in *The Coming Millennial Kingdom: A Case for Premillennial Interpretation*, eds. Donald K. Campbell & Jeffrey L. Townsend (Grand Rapids: Kregel, 1997),

"Evidence from Romans 9–11," by S. Lewis Johnson, Jr. in *The Coming Millennial Kingdom: A Case for Premillennial Interpretation*, eds. Donald K. Campbell & Jeffrey L. Townsend (Grand Rapids: Kregel, 1997), 199–224.

"Evidence from 1 Corinthians 15," by D. Edmond Hiebert in *The Coming Millennial Kingdom: A Case for Premillennial Interpretation*, eds. Donald K. Campbell & Jeffrey L. Townsend (Grand Rapids: Kregel, 1997), 225–234. (NOTE: Hiebert shows how 1 Corinthians 15 is consistent with a future millennial kingdom.)

"Evidence from Revelation," by Harold W. Hoehner in *The Coming Millennial Kingdom: A Case for Premillennial Interpretation*, eds. Donald K. Campbell & Jeffrey L. Townsend (Grand Rapids: Kregel, 1997), 235–262.

Future of Israel

The People, the Land, and the Future of Israel: Israel and the Jewish People in the Plan of God, eds., Darrell L. Bock and Mitch Glaser (Grand Rapids: Kregel, 2014).

Future Israel: Why Christian Anti-Judaism Must Be Challenged by Barry Horner (Nashville, TN: B&H, 2007).

"The Dispersion and Restoration of Israel to the Land," by John A. Jelinek in *Israel, the Land and the People: An Evangelical Affirmation of God's Promises*, ed. Wayne H. House (Grand Rapids: Kregel, 1998), 231–260.

"The Land of Israel and the Future Return (Zechariah 10: 6–12)," by Walter C. Kaiser, Jr. in *Israel, the Land and the People: An Evangelical Affirmation of God's Promises*, ed. Wayne H. House (Grand Rapids: Kregel, 1998), 209–230.

Israelology: The Missing Link in Systematic Theology by Arnold G. Fruchtenbaum (Tustin, CA: Ariel, 1994). (NOTE: The best book in print on Israel's past, present, and future.)

Has the Church Replaced Israel: A Theological Evaluation by Michael J. Vlach (Nashville, TN: B&H, 2010). (NOTE: While this book is a critique of replacement theology it offers much in regard to the future salvation and restoration of national Israel)

Rapture / Tribulation

Evidence for the Rapture: A Biblical Case for Pretribulationism, ed. John F. Hart (Chicago: Moody, 2015).

"Arguing for the Rapture: Who Must Prove What and How?" by John S. Feinberg in *When the Trumpet Sounds* (Eugene, OR: Harvest House, 1995), 187–210. (NOTE: This is not your average article on the rapture. Feinberg excels on the proper methodological approach for addressing the rapture issue.)

"Are the Church and the Rapture in Matthew 24?" by Stanley D. Toussaint in *When the Trumpet Sounds* (Eugene, OR: Harvest House, 1995), 235–250.

"The Olivet Discourse," by Thomas Ice in *The End Times Controversy: The Second Coming Under Attack*, eds. Tim LaHaye and Thomas Ice (Eugene, OR: Harvest House, 2003), 151–200.

"The 70 Weeks of Daniel," by Thomas Ice in *The End Times Controversy: The Second Coming Under Attack*, eds. Tim LaHaye and Thomas Ice (Eugene, OR: Harvest House, 2003), 307–354.

"The Little Apocalypse of Zechariah," by Arnold G. Fruchtenbaum in *The End Times Controversy: The Second Coming Under Attack*, eds. Tim LaHaye and Thomas Ice (Eugene, OR: Harvest House, 2003), 251–282.

"The Case for the Pretribulation Rapture Position," by Paul D. Feinberg in *Three Views on the Rapture*, ed. Stanley N. Gundry (Grand Rapids: Zondervan, 1984), 45–86.

Zionism / Current State of Israel

The Case for Christian Zionism: Why Christians Should Support Israel, by Thomas Ice (Green Forest, AR: New Leaf Press, 2017).

The New Christian Zionism: Fresh Perspectives on Israel & the Land, ed. Gerald R. McDermott (Downers Grove, IL: InterVarsity Press, 2016).